Grade 5

Wonders CALIFORNIA Content Reader

English Language Development

B

The McGraw·Hill Companies

Macmillan/McGraw-Hill

Published by Macmillan/McGraw-Hill, of McGraw-Hill Education, a division of The McGraw-Hill Companies, Inc., Two Penn Plaza, New York, New York 10121.

Printed in the United States of America

5 6 7 8 9 10 WEB 14 13 12 11

Contents

Contents

California History/Social Science Standards

Chemical Reactions

Matter is made of elements. An **element** is a simple substance. Elements are put together to make all other substances. Some common elements are carbon, aluminum, oxygen, and iron. Elements are different from one another. For example, some are heavy. Others are light.

Elements are made of tiny particles called atoms. An **atom** is the smallest particle that has the properties of an element. In fact, atoms are too small to see. That's because an atom is less than a billionth of an inch in size. Each element has one kind of atom. All atoms in an element are alike.

Matter is always changing. Liquid water can freeze into solid ice, for example. This change is called a physical change. The ice is not a new substance. It is just water in a solid form.

Chemical reactions are different. In a **chemical reaction**, a new substance is made. It is the result of a chemical change. What the substance starts out as is called a **reactant** (ree•AK•tuhnt). The new substance is called a **product.** To show that products come from reactants, we write it as

reactants → products

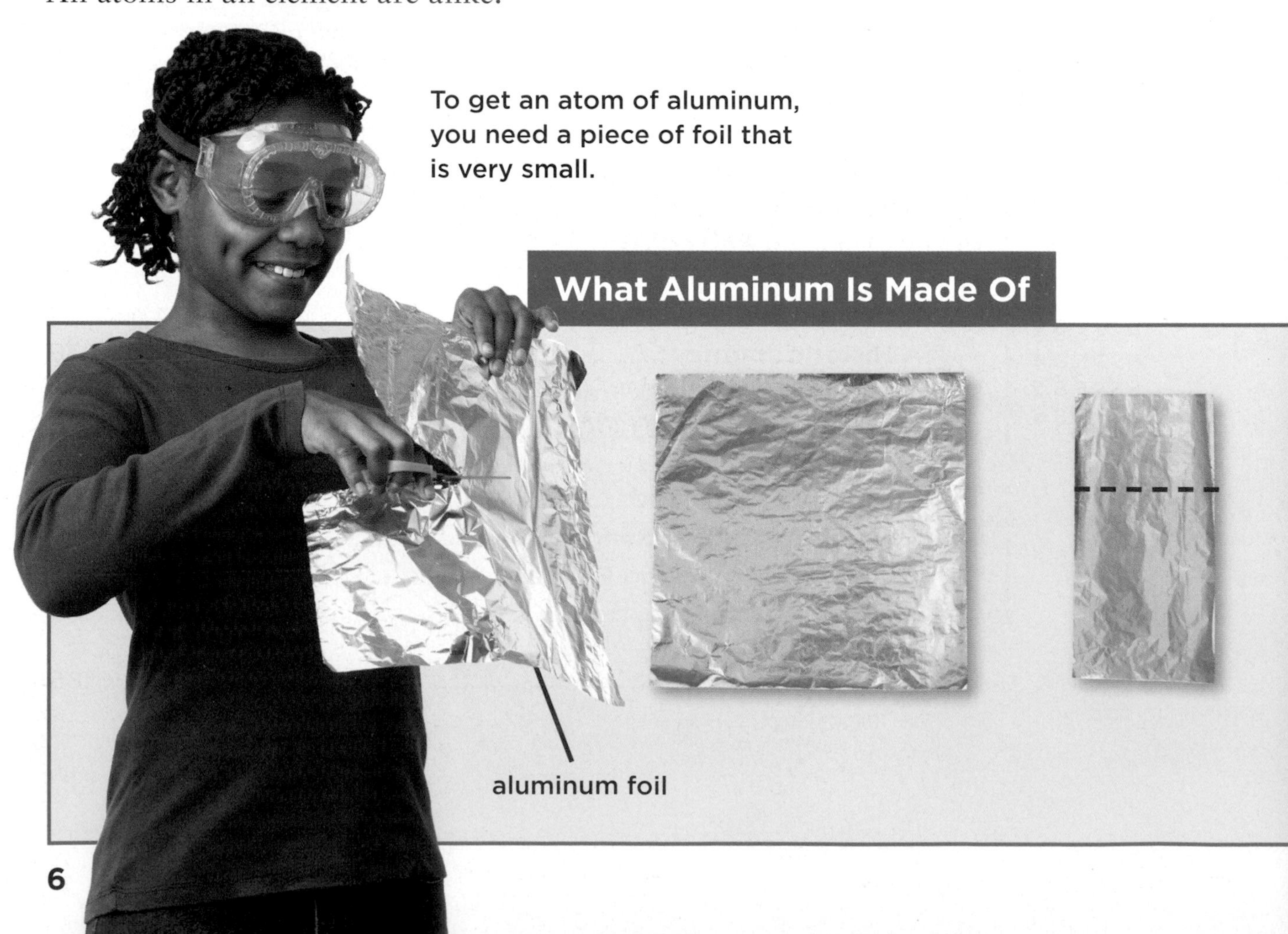

To get an atom of aluminum, you need a piece of foil that is very small.

A common example of a chemical reaction is the formation of carbon dioxide (CO_2). The diagram below shows how carbon (C) atoms and oxygen (O_2) molecules can combine. A molecule is a tiny particle made of one or more atoms. The reactants are carbon and oxygen. They combine into a product, carbon dioxide.

The total mass, or amount, of the products does not change. They have the same mass as the reactants before the chemical reaction. The total number of atoms also remained the same. For instance, three atoms are in the reactants and in the products shown below.

Atoms simply make new combinations. The new arrangement of atoms gives the products new and different properties. Atoms do not increase during chemical changes. They do not decrease, either.

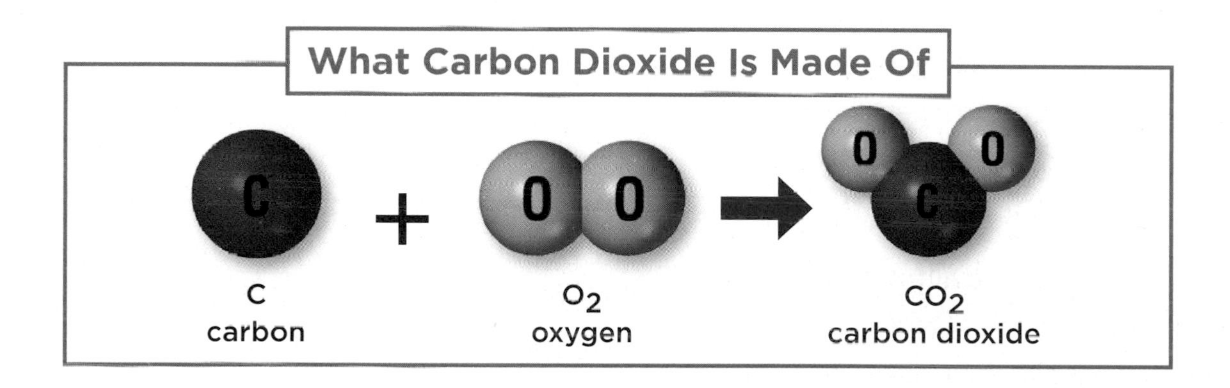

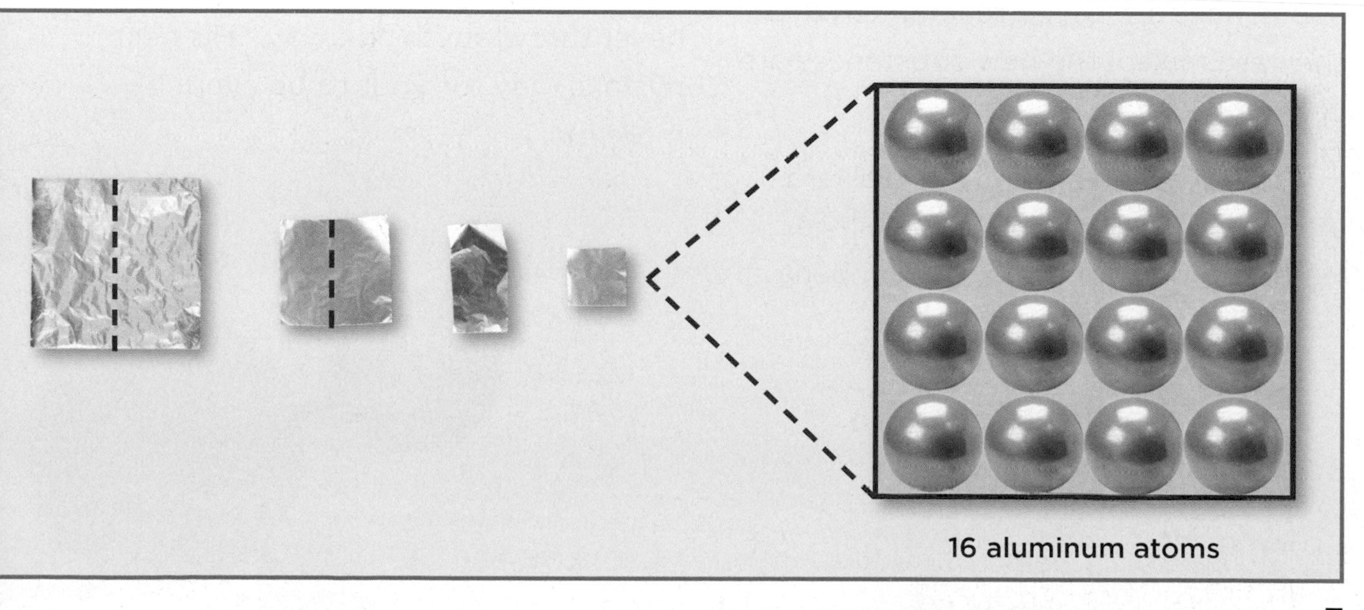

Mr. Mix-It

For one man, mixing chemistry and clay leads to new discoveries—toys!

Todd Bigelow/ Aurora

▲ **Chemist Maelo Cordova shows a slimy invention.**

Sometimes Maelo Cordova plays with modeling clay. Other times he tries out paint for dolls or races tiny cars. Cordova is a chemist. He uses chemistry to make toys.

As a kid in Puerto Rico, Cordova asked questions like, "How can I mix cleaning products to get out spots?" He loved learning how substances combine to make new stuff.

This process is called a chemical reaction. A chemical reaction occurs when two or more substances combine to make a new substance. The starting substances are called reactants. When they are mixed, the new substances are called products.

Cordova won a top science award. Then he studied chemistry in college. He now works for a big toy company.

At work, Cordova mixes chemicals and performs experiments. For one project, he was asked to make icky, sticky slime. The goo came out too hard, but he saved it. He later turned his mistake into a new invention, flubber. Says Cordova, "In science, you never throw anything away." His next mistake may turn out to be even more fun.

It's Elemental

Everything in the world is made of elements. An element is a substance that contains only one kind of atom. It can't be broken down into a simpler substance. A compound is made by combining two or more elements chemically. One compound is sodium chloride. It is a combination of the elements sodium and chlorine. You know it as table salt.

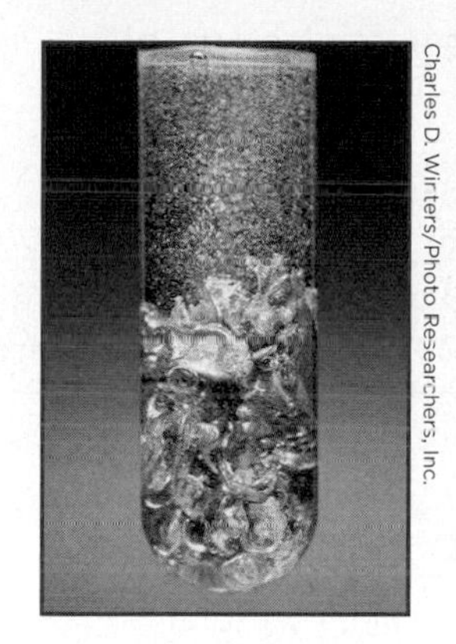

Charles D. Winters/Photo Researchers, Inc.

▲ Chemistry is all about combining elements.

TIME FOR KIDS

Light Up the Night

Some chemical reactions produce light. One example is a toy you may have seen. It is a plastic tube that glows in the dark. The tube is filled with a liquid substance. When you bend the tube, a small container inside it breaks. This causes a chemical reaction between the two substances. One product of the reaction is light. The light makes the dye in the tube glow in the dark.

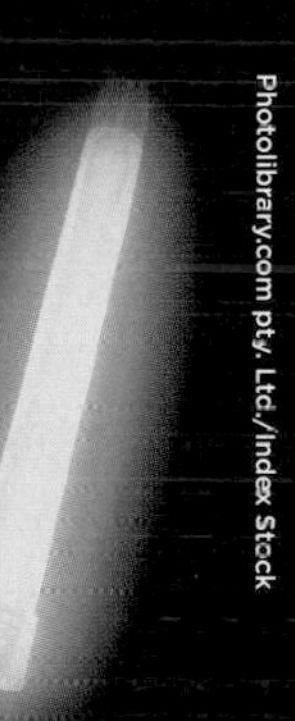

Photolibrary.com pty. Ltd./Index Stock

Great Chemistry

This table lists some famous chemists and their achievements.

Name	Birth Date	Country of Birth	Achievement
Robert Boyle	1627	England	First to use scientific methods to study chemistry
Irene Curie	1897	France	Made new radioactive elements
John Dalton	1766	England	Discovered theory of matter based on atoms
Antoine Lavoisier	1743	France	Discovered oxygen and that water is made of oxygen and hydrogen
Dimitri Mendeleyev	1834	Russia	Arranged all known elements in a chart called the periodic table
Alfred Nobel	1833	Sweden	Invented dynamite, an explosive

Description Writing Frame

Use the Writing Frame below to orally summarize "Chemical Reactions."

Elements are simple substances. They make up all other substances.

For example, some common elements are ____________________

____.

Elements are made of tiny invisible particles called ____________________.

During chemical reactions, the atoms in the reactants ____________________

____

____.

For example, a chemical reaction takes place between carbon (C) atoms and oxygen (O_2) molecules. The reactants, ____________________

____________________ are changed into the product ____________________

____.

Use the frame to write the summary on another sheet of paper. Be sure to include **bold** signal words. Keep this as a model of this Text Structure.

Critical Thinking

1 A starting substance in a chemical reaction is called a ________________.

A. reaction

B. product

C. reactant

2 Point to the sentence in "Mr. Mix-It" that tells what sodium chloride is.

3 Find the paragraph in "Chemical Reactions" that explains elements. Point to one common element.

4 What does the table on page 9 tell you about chemists? Discuss this table with a partner.

A table presents information such as names and numbers in a compact way.

Digital Learning

For a list of links and activities that relate to this Science standard, visit the California Treasures Web site at www.macmillanmh.com to access the Content Reader resources.

Have students view the Science in Motion Video "Formation of Carbon Dioxide."

In addition, distribute copies of the Translated Concept Summaries in Spanish, Chinese, Hmong, Khmer, and Vietnamese.

The Periodic Table

The **periodic table** shows all the known elements in a chart of rows and columns. The elements are placed in order by atomic number. The atomic number is shown in the top of each box. Different colors show the three different groups of elements. They are the metals, the metalloids, and the nonmetals.

The columns in the periodic table are called groups, or families. Families of elements have similar properties. The rows are called periods. Elements change from metals to nonmetals across the rows. Elements are more metal-like as you go down any family.

You may have noticed there are two rows that are not connected to the others. These rows include the rare earth elements. Many of these elements are synthetic, or human-made.

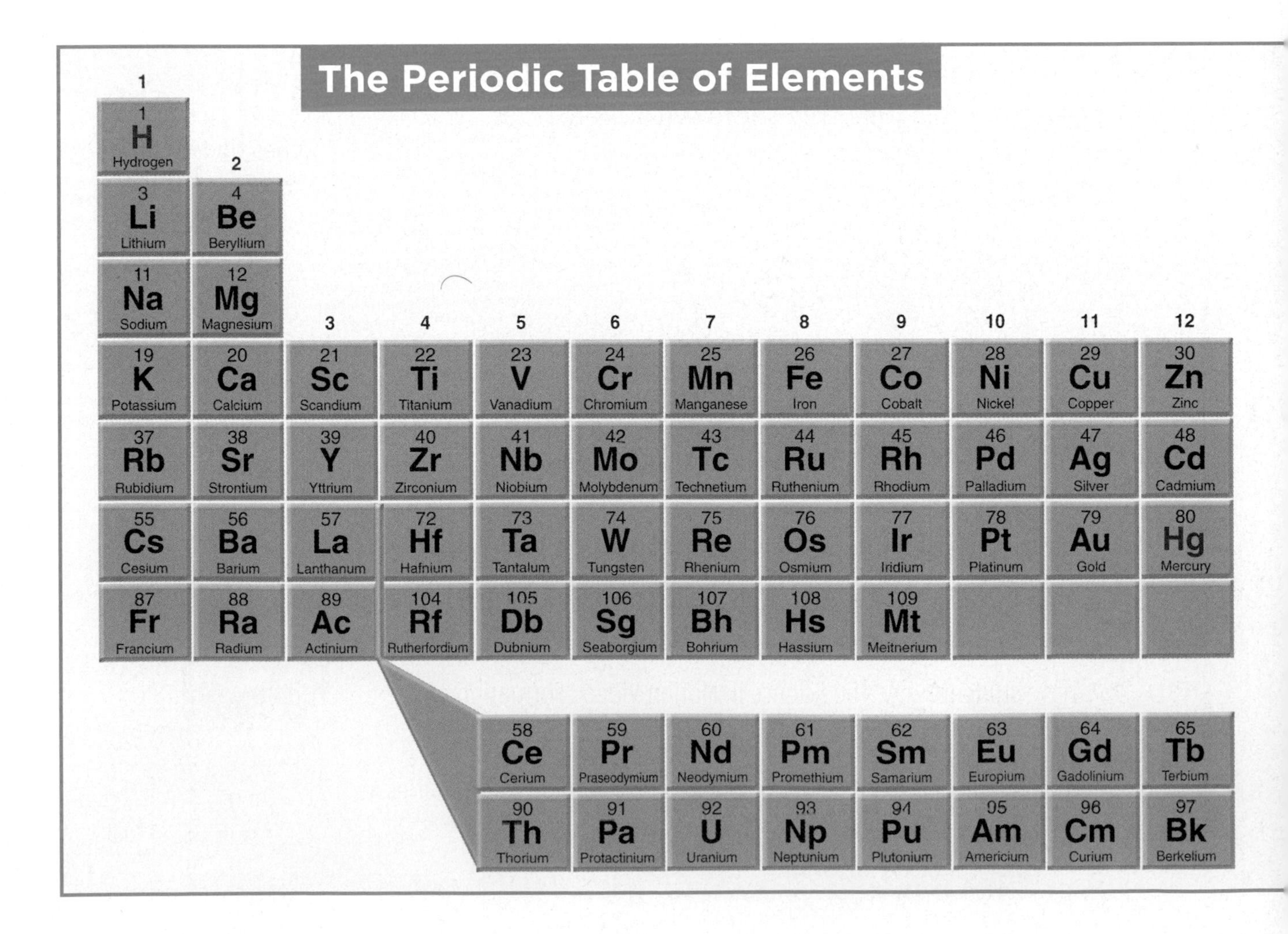

Most elements on the periodic table are metals. A **metal** is an element that is a good conductor of heat and electricity. That is, they let heat and electricity pass through them. Metals fill the left and center of the periodic table. They include gold (Au), copper (Cu), silver (Ag), zinc (Zn), aluminum (Al), iron (Fe), lead (Pb), mercury (Hg), magnesium (Mg), and chromium (Cr). When metals are polished, they shine.

Metals melt—become liquid—at different temperatures. This makes them useful for many purposes. Mercury, for example, is used in barometers. That is because it is a liquid at room temperature. The air pressure is measured by the height of the mercury column. Metals that melt at high temperatures are also useful. Aircraft and spacecraft, for example, often have metal parts that are made of titanium (Ti). This element can take the heat—titanium melts at 1,668°C (3,034°F)! It is also light and strong, good for a flying craft.

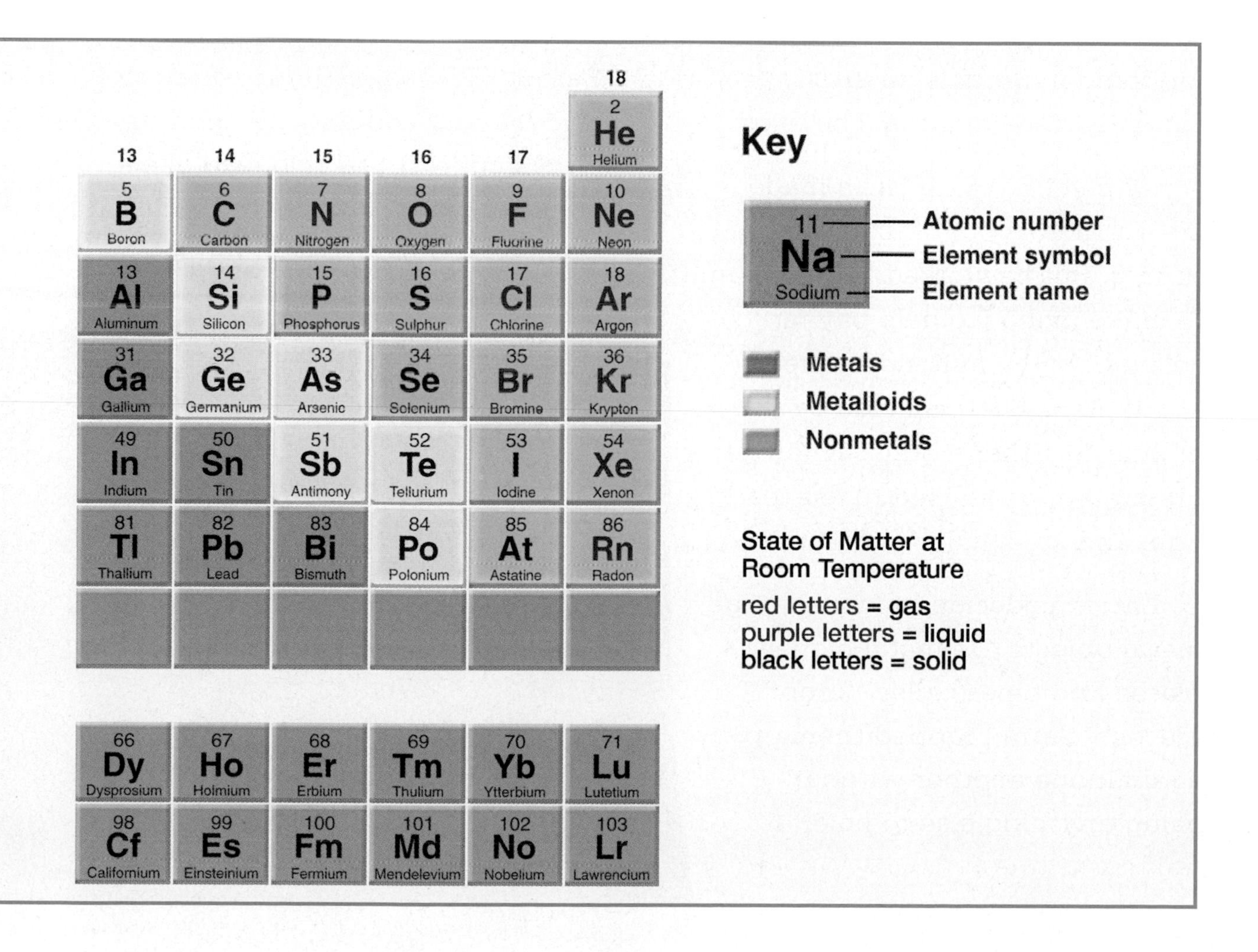

Richard Serra: *Artist*

Richard Serra and one of his works of art.

Ramin Talaie/Corbis

Some people use steel to make buildings or machines. Others use steel to make art.

Richard Serra used to throw hot lead at the wall. He won awards for doing it. Serra is an artist. Lead is just one of the materials he uses.

As a young man, Serra made his sculptures out of fiberglass and rubber. But he worked in a steel mill to make money to help pay for college. At the mill, he learned about steel. Steel is made by mixing together metals. When he graduated, he started to use lead, iron, and steel in his sculptures.

Later, he decided to make huge metal objects. He made big lead plates and pipes called "prop pieces." Serra propped them up against one another without using anything else to hold them up. One of the prop pieces was called "One Ton Prop (House of Cards)." It was just four squares of lead leaning against one another to form a cube. It really looked like a house of cards. It didn't fall. If it had, there would have been a huge crash!

Serra became more famous. He made sculptures for outdoor parks. He used big steel plates to build a series of sculptures called "Torqued Ellipse." These sculptures are made up of steel plates that are 13 feet high. There is a gap on one side to allow viewers to enter.

The sculptures were so popular that Serra was asked to come up with even more. He made huge steel spirals and rippling bands of steel.

Serra bends steel at high temperatures. Then he leaves it out in the rain. This gives the surfaces of his pieces a weathered look.

Before New York City's Museum of Modern Art could display Serra's sculptures, museum staff had to make sure the floors wouldn't fall in. After all, just one of Serra's pieces weighs 243 tons. (An average airplane weighs 199 tons!) *—Lisa Jo Rudy*

▼A museum visitor explores Serra's work from the inside.

▼Serra makes his sculptures by bending steel at very high temperatures.

Jose Sinal/epa/Corbis

Thos Robinson/Getty Images

Sequence Writing Frame

Use the Writing Frame below to orally summarize "Richard Serra: Artist."

Richard Serra is a famous artist. When he was young he **first** made

his sculptures out of ______________________________

______________________________.

Then ______________________________

______________________________ to help pay for college.

After college, Serra started working with ______________________________

______________________________.

Later, Serra decided to make sculptures that were ______________________________

______________________________.

Then Serra became more famous and he ______________________________

______________________________.

Today many people have explored Richard Serra's sculptures.

Use the frame to write the summary on another sheet of paper. Be sure to include the **bold** signal words. Keep this as a model of this Text Structure.

Critical Thinking

1. An element that is a good conductor of heat and electricity is ________________.

   A. magnet

   B. metal

   C. magnesium

2. Find the paragraphs in "The Periodic Table" that explains that metals melt at different temperatures.

3. Point to the sentence in "Richard Serra: Artist" that tells what happens when Serra leaves his steel out in the rain.

4. Discuss the periodic table on page 12 with a partner. What do the colors of the boxes and letters mean?

A table presents information such as names and numbers in a compact way.

Digital Learning

For a list of links and activities that relate to this Science standard, visit the California Treasures Web site at www.macmillanmh.com to access the Content Reader resources.
Have students view the e-Review "Metals and Alloys."
In addition, distribute copies of the Translated Concept Summaries in Spanish, Chinese, Hmong, Khmer, and Vietnamese.

Mixtures and Microscopes

A **mixture** (MIKS•chuhr) is a combination of two or more substances that do not form new substances.

The properties of a mixture blend the properties of its parts. For example, muddy water is a mixture of clay and water. Powdery clay alone can get you dirty and water alone can get you wet. On the other hand, the mixture can get you both dirty *and* wet.

We group mixtures according to their properties. In heterogeneous mixtures, particles from all substances are big enough to see. Trail mix and tossed salad are examples of heterogeneous mixtures.

Mixtures that look the same throughout are homogenous mixtures. In homogeneous mixtures, the particles are too small to see. Milk and cream cheese are examples of homogeneous mixtures. They look the same throughout because you can't see the individual particles.

Some mixtures settle and separate by themselves. We call this type of mixture a **suspension** (suh•SPEN•shuhn). In some suspensions, particles settle into layers quickly. Oil and vinegar as a salad dressing, for example, can be shaken together to make a smooth-looking mixture. However, the oil forms a layer on top of the vinegar in minutes.

If the particles in a mixture are very small the mixture is called a **solution** (suh•LEW•shuhn). This happens when one substance dissolves in another, like sugar in water. All solutions are homogeneous. That is, they have the same makeup throughout.

After they are mixed together and left to sit, oil and vinegar separate into two layers.

The field ion microscope was invented in 1951. Atoms appear as bright spots.

The particles in some mixtures are very small. In a pinch of salt there are more than a billion particles the size of atoms. Half of them are sodium particles and half are chlorine particles. They are much too small for us to see with just our eyes.

However, microscopes allow scientists to "see" atoms. An **electron microscope** aims electrons at a sample. Electrons are particles even smaller than atoms. When an electron hits an atom and bounces back, an image is formed. The first electron microscope was invented in 1932.

The **field ion microscope** was invented in 1951. Instead of electrons it uses ions to form images. Ions are particles with an electric charge. The field ion microscope is even more powerful than the electron microscope. It helped scientists to see atoms, not large molecules, like the electron microscope.

This technology shows that metal atoms are shaped like a ball. Studying how these particles act helps scientists understand smaller parts inside the atom. These parts are protons, neutrons, and electrons.

The field ion microscope only shows large atoms and molecules. However, a new microscope has helped to solve this problem. The scanning tunneling microscope uses a very fine metallic tip to examine samples.

Name That Powder

A laser light invention helps keep Americans safe.

Ever since the destruction of the World Trade Center in 2001, the United States has been watching for terrorism. The Department of Homeland Security looks for anything that could harm American citizens.

In 2001, someone mailed a harmful substance called anthrax to several members of Congress and TV anchors. A number of postal workers got sick. Several even died.

Homeland Security helps when unidentified powders and mixtures turn up. The powder could be harmless but it could also be very dangerous.

Up until now, Homeland Security had to send a sample to a laboratory. Days or weeks later, they'd get an answer. This could be a very long wait if people were sick and in need of help. How could Homeland Security figure it out more quickly?

AP Photo

Special clothing protects workers who handle unidentified substances.

The answer might be a device called the Raman spectrometer. Raman spectrometers direct laser light at an object or substance's molecules. Laser light is a very strong beam of light. The light from the laser bounces back. Some of the light changes color. The Raman spectrometer identifies the object or substance by matching its color to a library of "light signatures."

One company has taken the Raman spectrometer out of the lab. The machine can be carried around and powered with batteries. Its inventor, Daryoosh Vakhshoori, says you can use it to "read the substance as if it had a bar code, observing if the white powder you see is sugar, aspirin, or something dangerous."

The portable device helped after Hurricane Katrina hit New Orleans, Louisiana. Sludge was everywhere. Cleanup crews used the machine to learn what was in the sludge. Now, a new system called SORS (spatially offset Raman spectroscopy) can identify molecules that are inside items such as luggage and other bags. Raman spectrometers may be at work at an airport or on city streets right now. *—Lisa Jo Rudy*

Jason Grow

▲ **Daryoosh Vakhshoori and his portable spectrometer.**

M Kane/San Antonio Express-News/ZUMA Press

Sludge left by Hurricane Katrina could have made people and animals sick. ▶

Compare/Contrast Writing Frame

Use the Writing Frame below to orally summarize "Mixtures and Microscopes."

A mixture is ____

____.

The properties of a mixture blend ____________________________.

However, there are different types of mixtures. In heterogeneous

mixtures, the particles ____________________________________

____.

In homogeneous mixtures, the particles _______________________

____.

There is another way mixtures are **different**. In a mixture called a

____________, the particles settle and separate within a few hours.

In **contrast**, in a solution ______________________________.

So, mixtures have similarities and differences.

• • • • • • • • • • • • • • • • •

Use the frame to write the summary on another sheet of paper. Be sure to include **bold** signal words. Keep this as a model of this Text Structure.

Critical Thinking

1 An electron microscope uses ________________ to produce images.

A. light

B. heat

C. electron beams

2 Find the kind of microscope from "Mixtures and Microscopes" that scientists use to "see" atoms.

3 Point to the place in the text "Name That Powder" where it talks about how long it took for labs to get information to Homeland Security.

4 Refer to the photo on page 20 and discuss with a partner how the caption helps you understand the text.

Photographs and captions help you understand facts in an informational article.

Digital Learning

For a list of links and activities that relate to this Science standard, visit the California Treasures Web site at www.macmillanmh.com to access the Content Reader resources.

Have students view the e-Review "Mixtures."

In addition, distribute copies of the Translated Concept Summaries in Spanish, Chinese, Hmong, Khmer, and Vietnamese.

The States of Matter

Look at all the matter around you. Books, tables, air, milk, oil, and raindrops are made of matter.

As you know, these items are not alike. They are not the same **state of matter**. A state of matter is one of the three forms that matter can take. They are solid, liquid, and gas.

Books and tables are examples of solids. Milk, oil, and raindrops are liquids. Tires, balloons, basketballs, and your classroom contain gas. All matter is made of tiny particles. How the particles act tells the state of matter.

The particles of a solid usually line up in a pattern. They do not move past one another. They "wiggle" in place. The diagram of the solid shows its particles. They are packed together tightly, with no room between them. This is why the shape and volume of a solid do not change.

The particles of a liquid move more than they do in the solid state. They can move around more and even pass one another. However, they stay fairly close together.

The diagram of the liquid shows how particles in a liquid act. Since the particles of a liquid can flow, liquid takes on the shape of its container. If there is no container, the liquid spreads out as far as it can. The volume of a liquid stays the same no matter how far it spreads out.

Gases have particles that move very rapidly. The particles have lots of empty space between them. They move faster when hot and slower when cool.

In the gas diagram, the particles move around freely. They fit the shape and volume of the container. If there is no container, gases keep spreading further and further apart.

solid

liquid

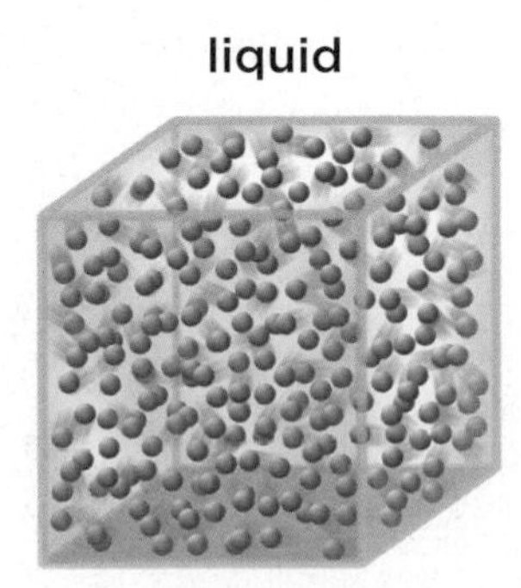

gas

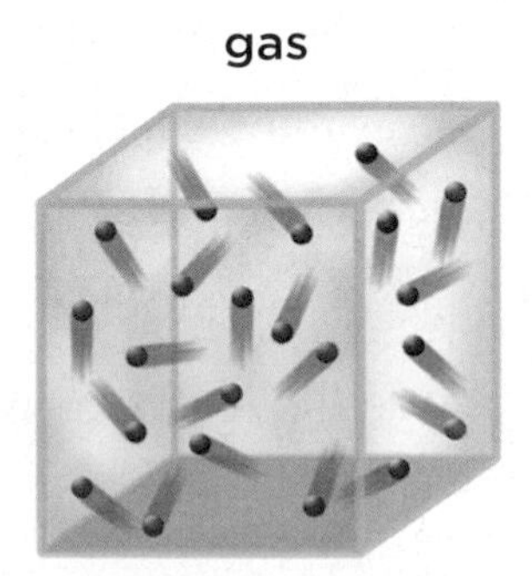

Common Elements

All living things share common elements. Plants have thick cell walls and many woody parts that are made mainly of carbon, hydrogen, and oxygen.

Like plants, animals are made mainly of carbon, hydrogen, and oxygen. Animal bodies contain a lot of water. In fact, about 60% of human body weight is water. Water is made up of two elements—hydrogen and oxygen. Other than bones and teeth, the rest of our bodies are mostly carbon, oxygen, hydrogen, nitrogen, phosphorus, and a dash of chlorine and sulfur. So really, carbon, hydrogen, and oxygen are three elements shared by all plants and animals.

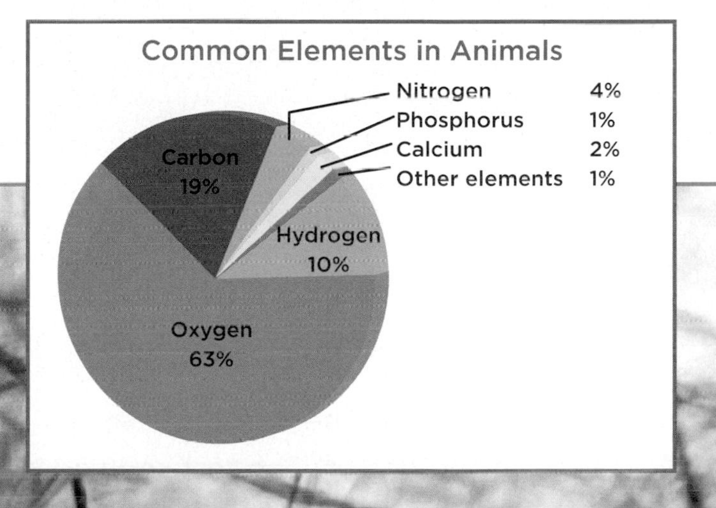

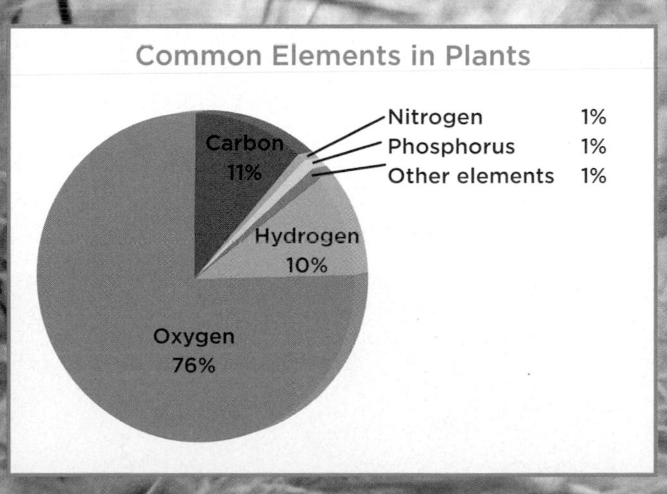

▼ Plants and animals are made mainly of carbon, hydrogen, and oxygen.

New Clues to a Mystery

Mystery still surrounds the circle of massive stones at Stonehenge.

An ancient mystery has puzzled people for hundreds of years.

Peter Adams/Getty Images

The Stonehenge World Heritage site is in southern England. Stonehenge is a circle of large, standing stones. We know that the stones line up with the Sun on the first day of summer and winter. However, Stonehenge remains a puzzle. No one knows exactly how it was built. The huge stones each weigh several tons. The people who built Stonehenge had to move them long distances. Archaeologists have now found a major piece of the puzzle.

Prehistoric Homes

The puzzle piece is a very old village. Scientists found it buried in the ground about two miles from Stonehenge. So far, they dug up the floors of eight wooden houses, along with tools and bones. Scientists believe the villagers built Stonehenge.

The scientists wanted to know how old the items are. They used a test called carbon dating. The test showed that the village is about the same age as Stonehenge. Both are about 4,500 years old.

▼ **Scientists have found the remains of an ancient village near Stonehenge.**

Adam Stanford/Aerial-Cam

Radioactive Carbon (C-14) and Carbon Dating

Plants get radioactive carbon (C-14) from the air. When animals eat the plants, C-14 enters the animals' bodies. Humans take in C-14 by eating animals and plants. Our bodies contain the same percentage of C-14 atoms as all living plants and animals have.

When a plant, animal, or human dies, it stops taking in C-14. The C-14 that is in it decays slowly. Scientists know exactly how long it takes for C-14 to decay. When they measure the amount of C-14 left in something, they can figure out how old the object is. Objects can be up to 50,000 years old and still be measured.

James Patterson

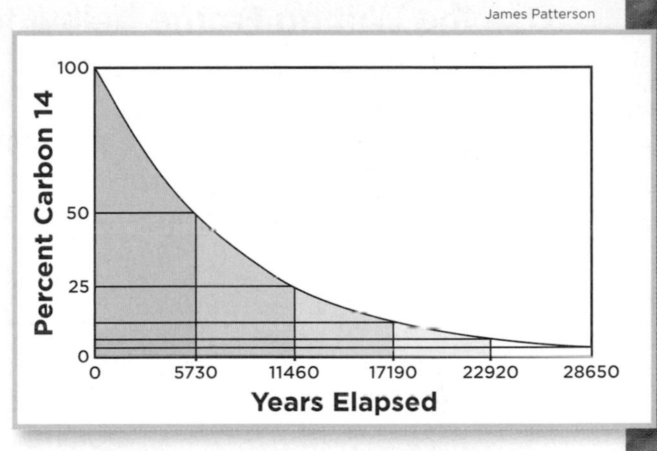

▲ **The amount of C-14 in something that once lived reveals how long ago it died.**

Connecting the Dots

The ancient village is in an area known as Durrington Walls. Both Stonehenge and Durrington Walls have stone avenues that lead to the Avon River. (See the map.) People could have used the river to travel from one place to the other. Researchers think that Stonehenge was a religious site.

"We knew these [sites] were from broadly the same period," says Julian Thomas, the project's director. Scientists have learned that the sites were closely connected. "[That] completely changes our understanding of Stonehenge."

Time For Kids

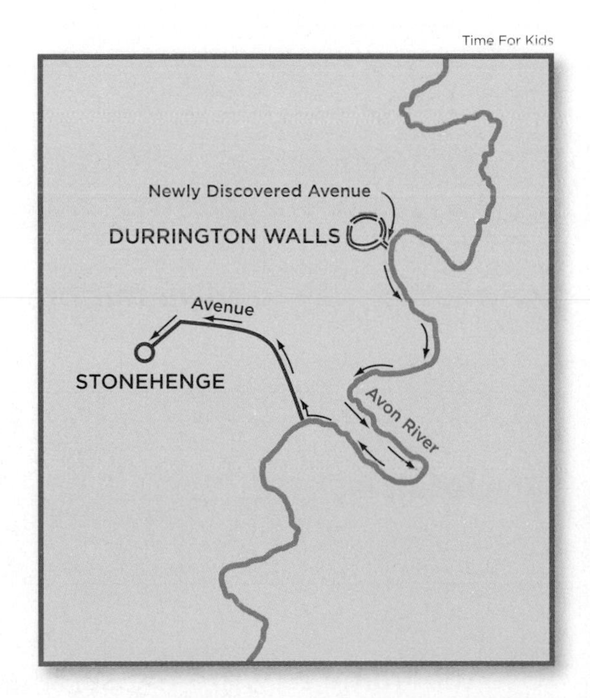

▲ **This map shows how people might have used the Avon River to travel between the ancient village and Stonehenge.**

Problem/Solution Writing Frame

Use the Writing Frame below to orally summarize "New Clues to a Mystery."

Scientists want to solve the mystery of Stonehenge.

The **problem** is no one knows how ______________________________

____

because the people had to move ______________________________

____.

To help solve this problem, a scientific team dug up ______________

____.

They found ______________________________________

____.

As another way to **solve this** problem, scientists used ______________

______________________ to see how old the village was.

The **result** is ______________________________________

____.

Use the frame to write the summary on another sheet of paper. Be sure to include the **bold** signal words. Keep this as a model of this Text Structure.

Critical Thinking

1 Which is not the name of a state of matter?

A. air

B. liquid

C. solid

2 Find the sentence in "New Clues to a Mystery" that explains how humans take in radioactive carbon.

3 Point out the paragraph in "The State of Matter" that describes how particles in a liquid act.

4 How does the map on page 27 support the text of "New Clues to a Mystery?"

Maps are drawings of geographic locations such as a city, state, or park.

Digital Learning

For a list of links and activities that relate to this Science standard, visit the California Treasures Web site at www.macmillanmh.com to access the Content Reader resources.

Have students view the e-Review "Properties of Matter."

In addition, distribute copies of the Translated Concept Summaries in Spanish, Chinese, Hmong, Khmer, and Vietnamese.

Plant and Animal Cells

All living things are made of cells. A **cell** (SEL) is the smallest unit of a living thing that can carry out the basic processes of life. Cells make up grass and mountain lions. Cells are tiny building blocks. Your own body is built of trillions of them.

▼ This mountain lion and the grass are made of many cells.

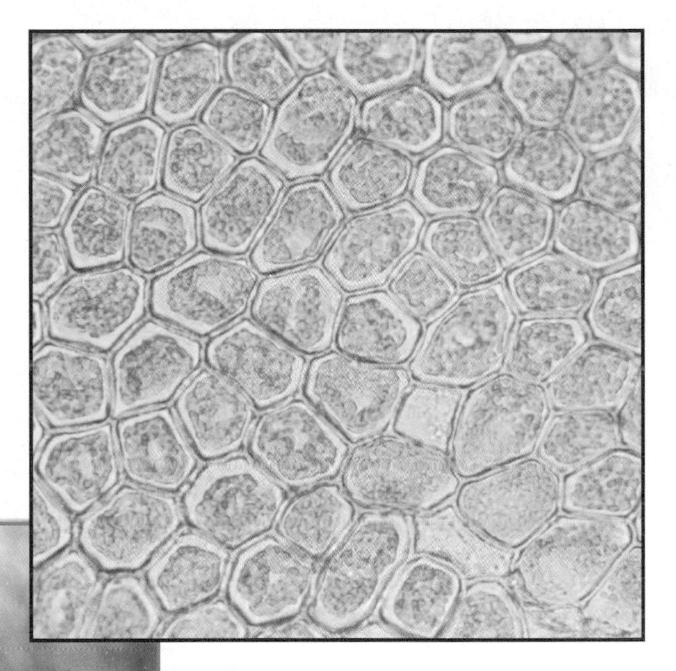

▲plant cell

Cells found in different living things have many things in common. All cells need energy to carry out life processes. All cells have structures, called **organelles** (awr•guh•NELZ). Organelles work together to help cells perform life processes. Organelles keep the cell alive.

Think about how plants and animals are different. Animals move around, but plants stay in one place. Animals look for water and food to take in. They eat other living things. Plants must store water and make their own food. Plants need to reach and use sunlight.

For these reasons, plant and animal cells are not the same. Plant cells give the plant support to stand tall. They also can store water to use later. Plant cells have special organelles that produce food. Animal cells do not need to store much water or produce food. However, animal cells need to be more flexible than plant cells because animals move around a lot.

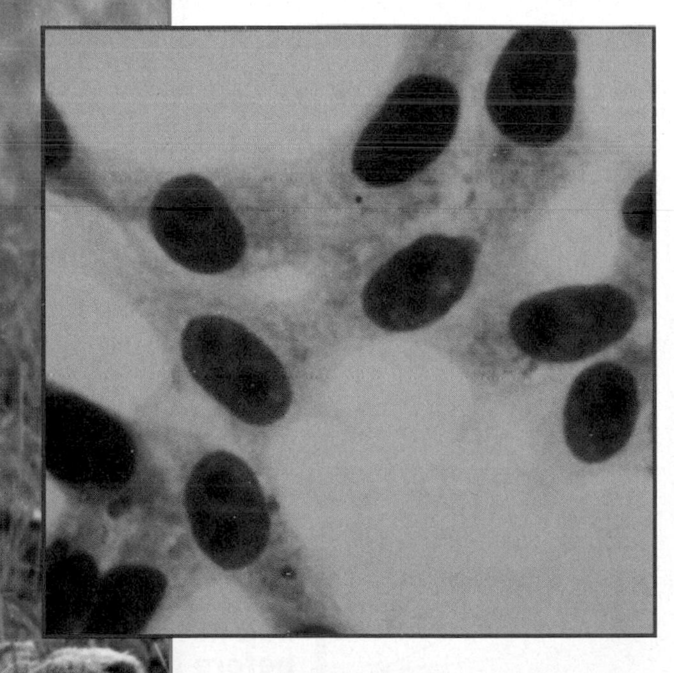

▲animal cell

A DINO BONE BREAKTHROUGH

How are a *T. rex* dinosaur and a chicken alike? Scientists may have the answer.

In 2003, scientists in Montana dug up a *Tyrannosaurus rex* (*T. rex*) fossil. A fossil is any remains of a dead plant or animal from long ago. This *T. rex* fossil was 70 million years old. When alive, it stood 40 feet tall and probably weighed five tons. Its thighbone was huge.

A Very Lucky Break

To fit the thighbone onto a helicopter, scientists had to break it in half. They took the *T. rex* bone into their lab at North Carolina State University. They got a surprise when they looked inside the bone. Over time, the soft and hard parts of the bones of dead animals disappear. This bone had a clear stretchy material inside. "It was totally shocking," said team leader Mary Schweitzer. Such material had never before been found in a dinosaur bone.

Under a very strong microscope, scientists examined the stretchy material. They saw tiny blood vessels and reddish-brown dots. They believe these dots are the nuclei, or central structures, of blood cells.

"Bone is living tissue (groups of cells), . . . and has to have a blood supply," said Schweitzer. The scientists saw what looked like bone-building cells. Bone cells rebuild bone tissues all the time.

Tissue from the *T. rex* thighbone returns to its original shape after being stretched.

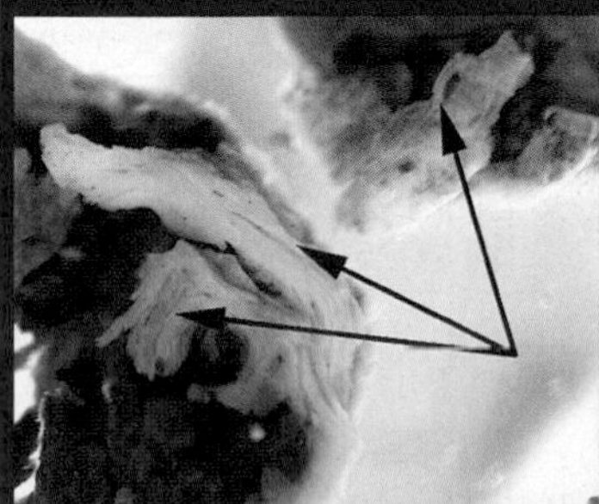

Areas of the bone have bundled strands of tissue which had never before been seen in such an old fossil.

(tl) AP Photo (bl) AP Photo

John Weinstein/
The Field Museum

T. Rex's Descendants

The *T. rex* thighbone gives new clues about dinosaurs. Scientists reported that its blood vessels are a lot like those in modern ostrich bones. This could support the theory that today's birds came from dinosaurs.

Another team of scientists studied material from the *T. rex* thighbone. They think *T. rex* is related to another modern bird—the chicken! "Based on the small sample we've recovered, chickens may be the closest relatives [to *T. rex*]," says John Asara, co-leader of the team. They also believe frogs and newts are modern relatives of *T. rex*.

A Real-Life Jurassic Park?

Some researchers hope to find dinosaur DNA in the *T. rex* thighbone materials. DNA is the chemical that makes up genes. Genes have the code for passing traits from parents to their offspring. Could the DNA be used to produce dinosaurs as in *Jurassic Park*?

Hans-Dieter Sues, a scientist who studies fossils, says no. "But," he adds, "there's lots of biological information locked in this material."

Dr. Schweitzer and her team of scientists are investigating other dinosaur sites around the world. They hope to find more dinosaur fossils that contain tissue samples. ***—Joe McGowan***

Chickens may be *T. rex*'s closest living relatives. ▶

G.K. & Vikki Hart/Getty Images

Compare/Contrast Writing Frame

Use the Writing Frame below to orally summarize "Plant and Animal Cells."

The cells of plants and animals are **alike** in many ways. They are

alike because all cells need ______________________________.

They are also **alike** because they both have structures called

____.

In some ways, however, ______________________ and

______________________ are **different**. They are **different**

because plant cells ______________________________

____.

They are also **different** because animals need cells ______________

____.

So ______________________ and ______________________

cells are **alike** in some ways, but **different** in others.

Use the frame to write the summary on another sheet of paper. Be sure to include **bold** signal words. Keep this as a model of this Text Structure.

Critical Thinking

1 The smallest unit of a living thing that can carry out the basic processes of life is a ________________.

A. organelle

B. cell

C. atom

2 Point to the sentence in "A Dino Bone Breakthrough" that explains what the reddish brown dots might be.

3 Find the paragraph in "Plant and Animal Cells" that tells why animals need cells that are flexible.

4 Study the photographs on page 32. Discuss with a partner what the tissue samples might tell about the *T. rex*.

Photographs and captions help you understand content in an informational article.

Digital Learning

For a list of links and activities that relate to this Science standard, visit the California Treasures Web site at www.macmillanmh.com to access the Content Reader resources.

Have students view the Science in Motion Video "Cells to Organisms." In addition, distribute copies of the Translated Concept Summaries in Spanish, Chinese, Hmong, Khmer, and Vietnamese.

The Respiratory and Circulatory Systems

Your **respiratory system** carries the air you breathe. It moves gases between the air, your blood, and the rest of your body.

When you **inhale**, or breathe in, air enters your body. Your **lungs**, organs that fill with air when you inhale, grow like balloons. When you **exhale**, or breathe out, the air empties out of your lungs. A large, flat sheet of muscle called the **diaphragm** (DIGH•uh•fram) controls your breathing.

Tubes bring air to your lungs. The tubes have tiny blood vessels called **capillaries** all around them. Oxygen from the air in the tubes enters the blood cells in the capillaries. They take the oxygen to the rest of your cells.

As blood passes through the lungs, it takes in oxygen. The blood also gives off carbon dioxide, a product given off during cellular respiration. Carbon dioxide and water vapor leave the body when you exhale.

The heart, blood vessels, and blood make up the **circulatory system**. This system is also known as the cardiovascular system.

Your circulatory system is like a postal system for your body. Blood cells bring things to and from your body cells. Your heart, a muscular organ, constantly pumps blood through your body.

First, your heart pumps blood into your arteries (AHR•tir•eez). Blood mixes with oxygen. Then, an artery carries it away from your heart. Your organs, tissues, and cells take oxygen, food, and nutrients from your blood.

Oxygen and waste, like carbon dioxide, move in and out of your blood. They travel through the walls of your capillaries. From the capillaries, the blood carrying carbon dioxide moves into your veins. A vein takes the blood cells carrying carbon dioxide back to your heart.

Circulation and Respiration

Your circulatory and respiratory systems work together. They transport oxygen and carbon dioxide through your body.

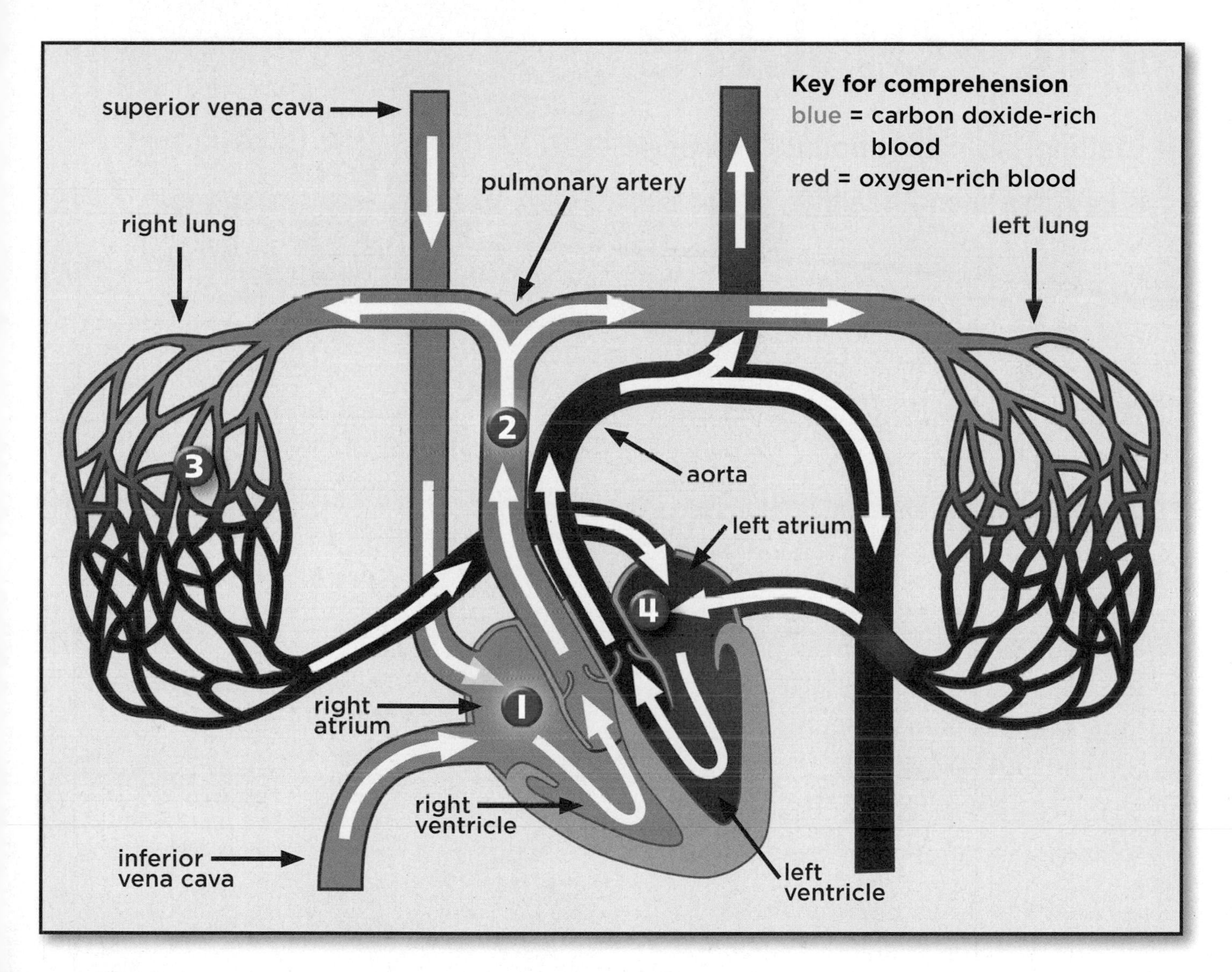

1. Carbon dioxide-rich blood from the superior vena cava and inferior vena cava enters the right atrium. Then the blood flows into the right ventricle. The pulmonary artery pumps out the blood.
2. The carbon dioxide-rich blood flows through the pulmonary artery. Then the blood enters the lungs.
3. In the lungs, the blood drops off carbon dioxide and picks up oxygen.
4. Oxygen-rich blood from the lungs flows through the pulmonary veins into the left atrium. Then the blood goes into the left ventricle, where the aorta pumps it out to the body.

How to Stay Fit for Life

Getting the right amount of exercise is key to staying healthy.

SW Productions/Photodisc/Getty Images

Kids are very busy. Health experts say most kids are not finding time to exercise.

"It's not true that kids get enough physical activity," gym teacher Andy Schmidt says.

This trend is part of the problem of unhealthy weight, or obesity, among kids. Many schools have cut down on gym and recess time. They are trying to save money or use the time to prepare students for tests.

Exercise helps build healthy bones, muscles, and joints. It keeps your body healthy. Exercise can also help kids avoid health problems like high blood pressure and heart disease when they get older.

The good news: Fun activities such as riding bikes or in-line skating with friends count. "Have fun, and do what you enjoy," Schmidt says. *—Ritu Upadhyay*

Many kids today don't get enough exercise. ▼

Corbis

A Formula for Staying Fit

The human body requires different types of exercise. Here are combinations for staying strong and flexible.

Todd Bigelow/Aurora/Getty Images

AEROBIC EXERCISE

Running, basketball, jumping rope, dancing

BENEFIT

Makes your heart and lungs strong and helps oxygen and blood move throughout your body.

AMOUNT

Thirty minutes a day, five days a week

Michelle Pedone/zefa/Corbis

STRENGTH TRAINING

Pull-ups, sit-ups, push-ups, tug-of-war

BENEFIT

Builds muscle strength and endurance, which improves overall physical fitness.

AMOUNT

Two or three days a week

MM Productions/Corbis

FLEXIBILITY TRAINING

Sit and reach, yoga, gymnastics, Tai Chi

BENEFIT

Flexibility allows you to move joints and stretch muscles fully.

AMOUNT

Before and after any workout

Julie Toy/Getty Images

More than half of girls and one quarter of boys ages 6 to 17 cannot run a mile any faster than they can walk a mile.

Cause/Effect Writing Frame

Use the Writing Frame below to orally summarize "How to Stay Fit for Life."

There are **several reasons** many young people do not exercise enough.

One reason is ______________________________.

Another reason is schools have ______________________________

______________________________.

This explains why there is a problem of ______________________________ among kids.

Exercising helps build ______________________________

______________________________.

It also helps kids avoid ______________________________

______________________________ when they get older.

For all of these reasons, it is important that kids ______________________________

______________________________.

Use the frame to write the summary on another sheet of paper. Be sure to include the **bold** signal words. Keep this as a model of this Text Structure.

Critical Thinking

1 A tiny blood vessel is a ________________.

A. vein

B. artery

C. capillary

2 Point to the sentence in "How to Stay Fit for Life" that tells the benefit of strength training.

3 Find the paragraph in "The Respiratory and Circulatory Systems" that explains what happens when you inhale and exhale.

4 What does the diagram on page 37 of "The Respiratory and Circulatory Systems" tell you about your body? Discuss it with a partner.

Diagrams help readers see, or visualize, difficult information in a text.

Digital Learning

For a list of links and activities that relate to this Science standard, visit the California Treasures Web site at www.macmillanmh.com to access the Content Readers resources.

Have students view the Science in Motion, "Circulation and Respiration."

In addition, distribute copies of the Translated Concept Summaries in Spanish, Chinese, Hmong, Khmer, and Vietnamese.

The Digestive System

Your cells need energy. They get this energy from the food you eat. Eating is like putting gas in a car. However, the food you eat is too big and complex for your tiny cells. **Digestion** breaks down the food into smaller and simpler substances. Your cells can then absorb the food your body digests.

Your body breaks down food. When you take a bite of food, your teeth chew it into smaller pieces. The salivary glands in your mouth and throat produce **saliva,** a watery fluid. Saliva helps to moisten and soften the chewed food, or bolus. It also helps break the food down.

Next, your tongue helps move the bolus to the **pharynx**, the part of the throat that connects the mouth to the digestive tube. Now you swallow. The bolus passes into a long, muscular tube called the **esophagus**.

The esophagus is slippery because it is lined with **mucus.** The walls of the esophagus contain muscles that squeeze the bolus along toward the **stomach.** It takes about ten seconds for a ball of food to move from the mouth to the stomach.

The stomach is a digestive organ with thick muscular walls. Three layers of muscles in the stomach squeeze the food. The muscles of the stomach contract and relax to move like a wave. The stomach adds mucus and digestive acids to the food. The muscles squeeze and mix the bolus for about four to six hours. The food, now a thick liquid, moves into the small intestine.

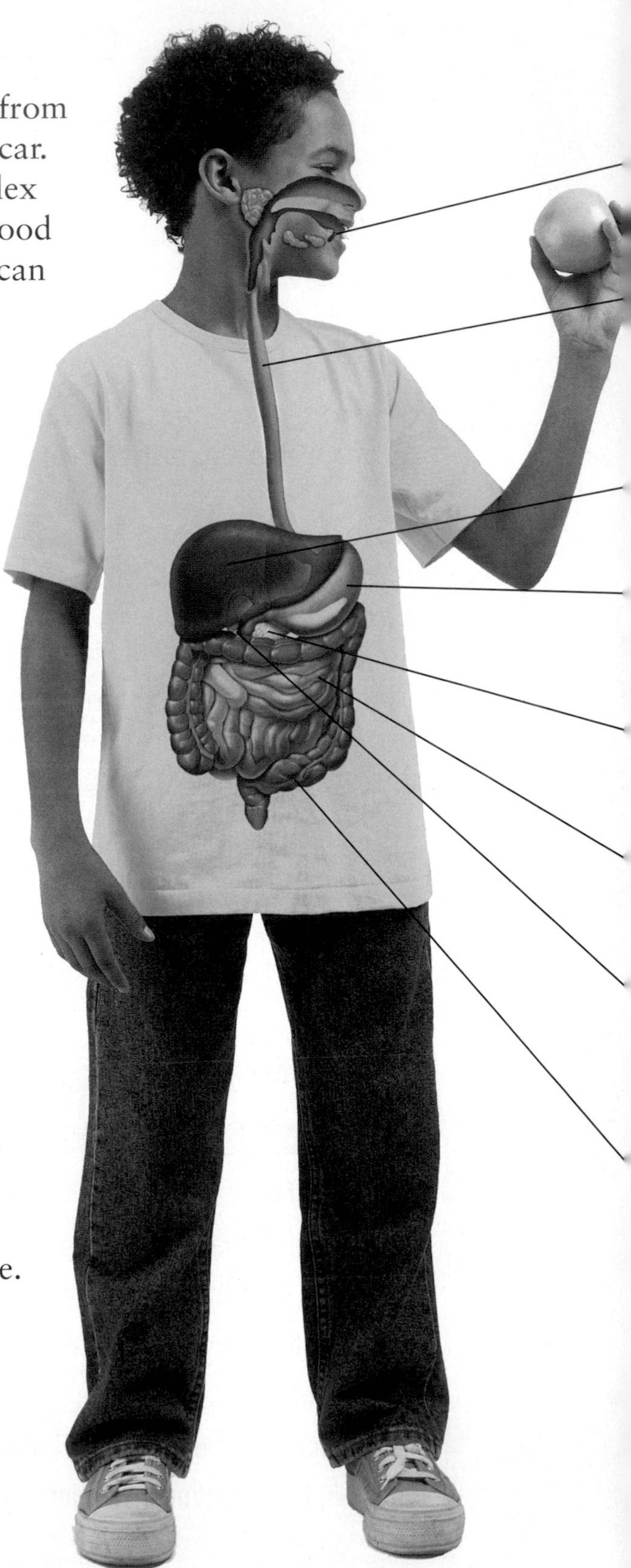

Mouth The mouth is where digestion begins.

Esophagus The esophagus is a tube that connects your mouth to your stomach.

Liver The liver adds digestive juices to food.

Stomach The stomach is a hollow bag with muscular walls.

Pancreas The pancreas is an organ about 6 inches long that produces several digestive juices.

Small Intestine The small intestine connects the stomach and the large intestine. It absorbs digested food.

Gall Bladder The gall bladder is a pear-shaped organ that stores digestive juices produced by the liver.

Large Intestine The large intestine eliminates undigested waste.

The **small intestine** is a coiled, tube-like organ that is connected to the stomach. In the small intestine, digestive juices break down the food into smaller, simpler forms. Nutrients from the food pass through the walls of the small intestine and into tiny blood vessels. Blood carries the nutrients to the rest of the body. The material that is left over moves on to the **large intestine**.

The large intestine is a thick, tubular organ. It removes undigested waste. It is shorter and thicker than the small intestine. The **cecum** connects the large intestine to the small intestine. The **colon** is the widest part of the large intestine. As waste passes through the colon, water and some minerals are absorbed and carried to your body tissue by the blood.

The last part of the large intestine is the **rectum**. The rectum stores solid waste called **feces**. Eventually, strong muscles push the feces out of the body through the **anus**. This process is called **elimination**.

The Photosynthesis and Respiration Cycle

All living things need energy. Plants and animals get energy in different ways. Plants' leaves capture and use energy from the Sun. Their roots absorb water. They take in carbon dioxide from the air. They use the energy, water, and carbon dioxide to make food. This food-making process is called photosynthesis.

The food plants produce during photosynthesis is sugar. Sugar is a **carbohydrate**, a substance made from carbon, hydrogen, and oxygen. Simple carbohydrates can be stored as food, used to make structural materials such as cell walls, or used for energy.

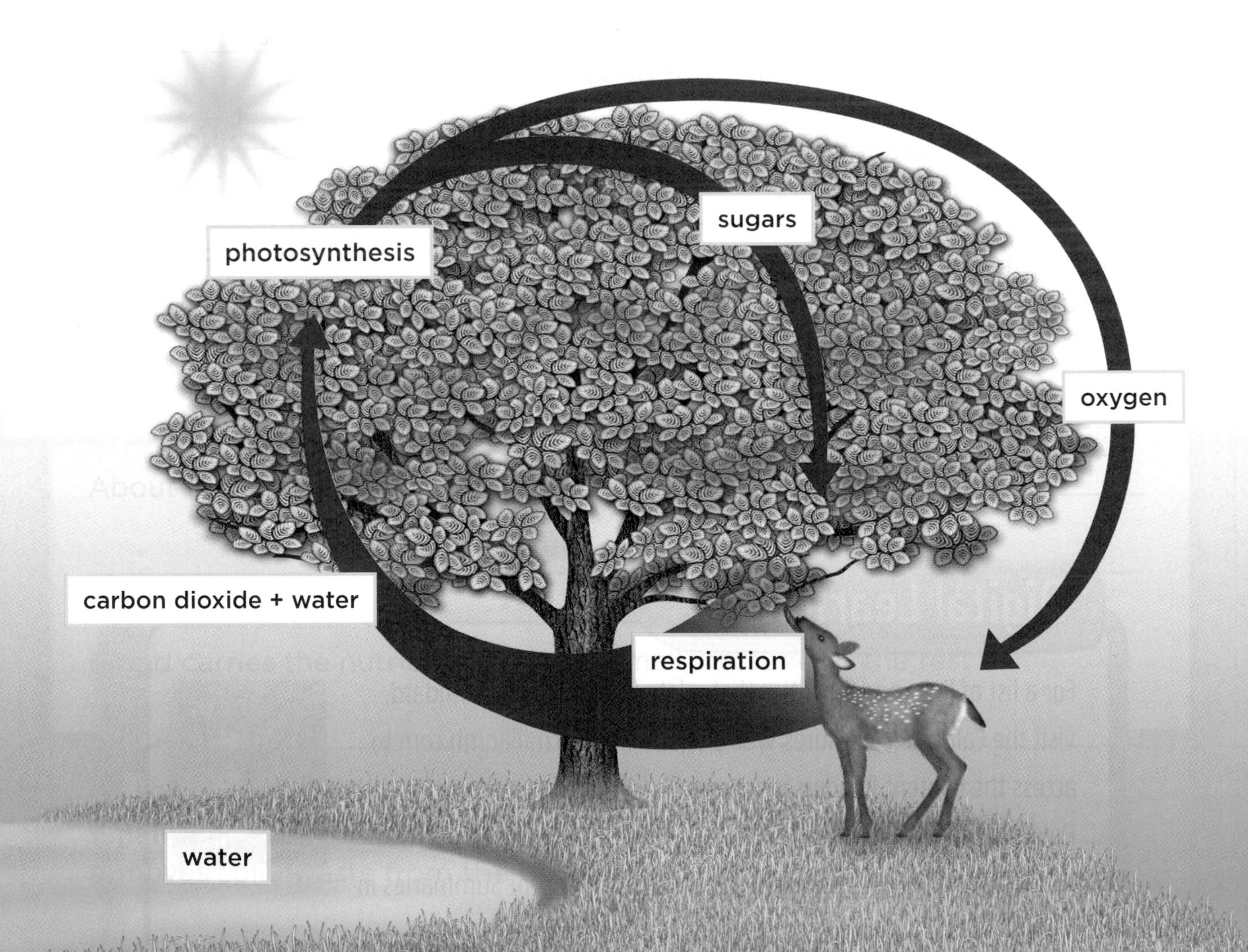

Like plants, animals depend on photosynthesis for energy. When an animal eats part of a plant, it takes in the carbohydrates stored in the plant. Even when animals are carnivores, animals that eat other animals, they take in the carbohydrates that the other animals got from eating plants.

You have learned that plants produce oxygen during photosynthesis. Animals take in oxygen during respiration. Plants also use some of the oxygen. Plant and animal cells use oxygen to break down stored carbohydrates to get energy. This process is called **cellular respiration**.

Compare photosynthesis and cellular respiration. Photosynthesis stores energy in food. Cellular respiration releases energy from food.

During cellular respiration, plant and animals cells produce carbon dioxide and water, which are then released back into the air. Plants use the carbon dioxide and water to produce food during photosynthesis. Then the cycle begins again.

Cellular respiration occurs in mitochondria, known as the power house of the cell. Mitochondria in plant and animal cells provide energy so cells can grow and repair themselves.

The mitochondria use oxygen to break down the stored carbohydrates to release energy. Carbon dioxide and water are also products of this reaction.

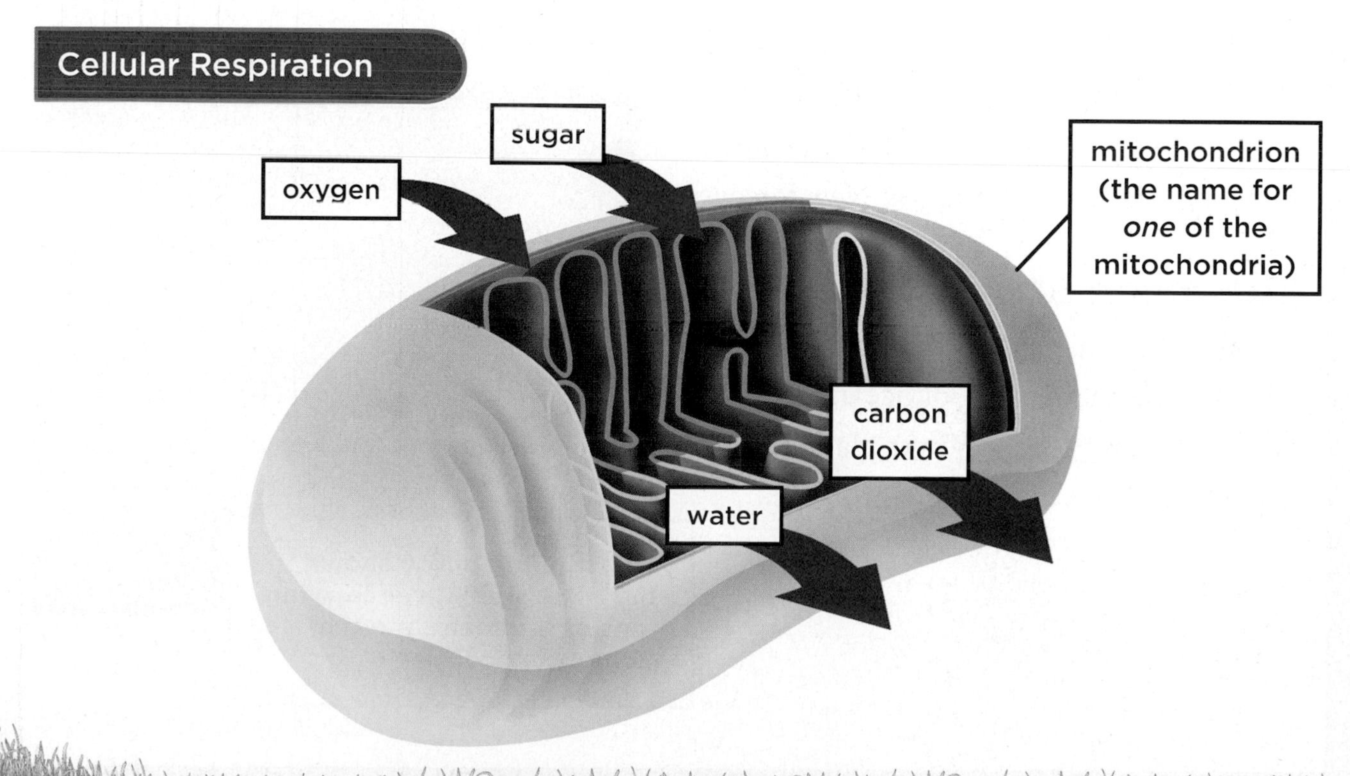

Are We Killing the Oceans?

Dead zones spread in the world's oceans.

The world's oceans are home to many living things, from microscopic organisms to whales, the largest animals on Earth. However, "dead zones" have been popping up in coastal waters around the globe. No animals live in these underwater areas because there is no oxygen. Without oxygen, fish and other animals cannot survive.

Over the past four decades, dead zones have appeared in almost 150 places, mostly in Europe and the East Coast of the United States. Some are small, but some are vast. The dead zone in the Gulf of Mexico is about the size of New Jersey.

Too Much of a Good Thing

Chemical fertilizer used on farms and lawns is the main cause of ocean dead zones. Pollution from power plants and other industries adds to the problem.

First, rain washes soil which has excess fertilizer and other chemicals into rivers. When rivers reach the ocean, all the chemicals flow in one spot. That's why ocean dead zones usually appear at the mouths of rivers.

When fertilizer reaches the oceans, tiny plant-like organisms called algae eat it. The well-fed algae grow, covering the surface of the ocean. When the algae die, they sink to the bottom of the ocean, where bacteria eat them.

This satellite photo shows the Mississippi River carrying tons of sediment into the Gulf of Mexico.

Pilar Olivares/Reuters/Corbis

Fertilizers and other chemicals can cause fish die-offs like this one.

The bacteria use oxygen and release carbon dioxide. With so much algae to eat, more and more bacteria grow. In time, the bacteria use up all the oxygen below the algae. With no oxygen, nothing can live at the bottom of the dead zones. There is too much life at the top.

Saving the Oceans

How can we keep dead zones from spreading? One solution is to plant trees and grasslands along rivers. The plants will soak up the fertilizer before it reaches the ocean. Reducing pollution from industry and untreated sewage can also help. Using less chemical fertilizer on farmlands and lawns can also help.

Algae blooms like this are a major reason ocean dead zones form.

Nati Harnik/AP Wide World Photo

Changing States of Water

Water covers most of Earth's surface. Most of this water can be found in oceans. An **ocean** is a large body of salt water. Oceans cover about 70 percent of Earth's surface. Land and other bodies of water take up the rest.

Water on Earth can take three forms, or states. Water you can pour into a glass is in the liquid state. Ice is water in the frozen state. Water vapor in the air is gas—that is, water in the gaseous state.

Where can you see water changing states? Think about the water in a pond. As fall turns to winter, the air temperature drops. Liquid water cools until it freezes into solid water, or ice. As winter turns to spring, the air temperature warms the frozen water. This makes ice melt.

Changes in State of Water in a Pond

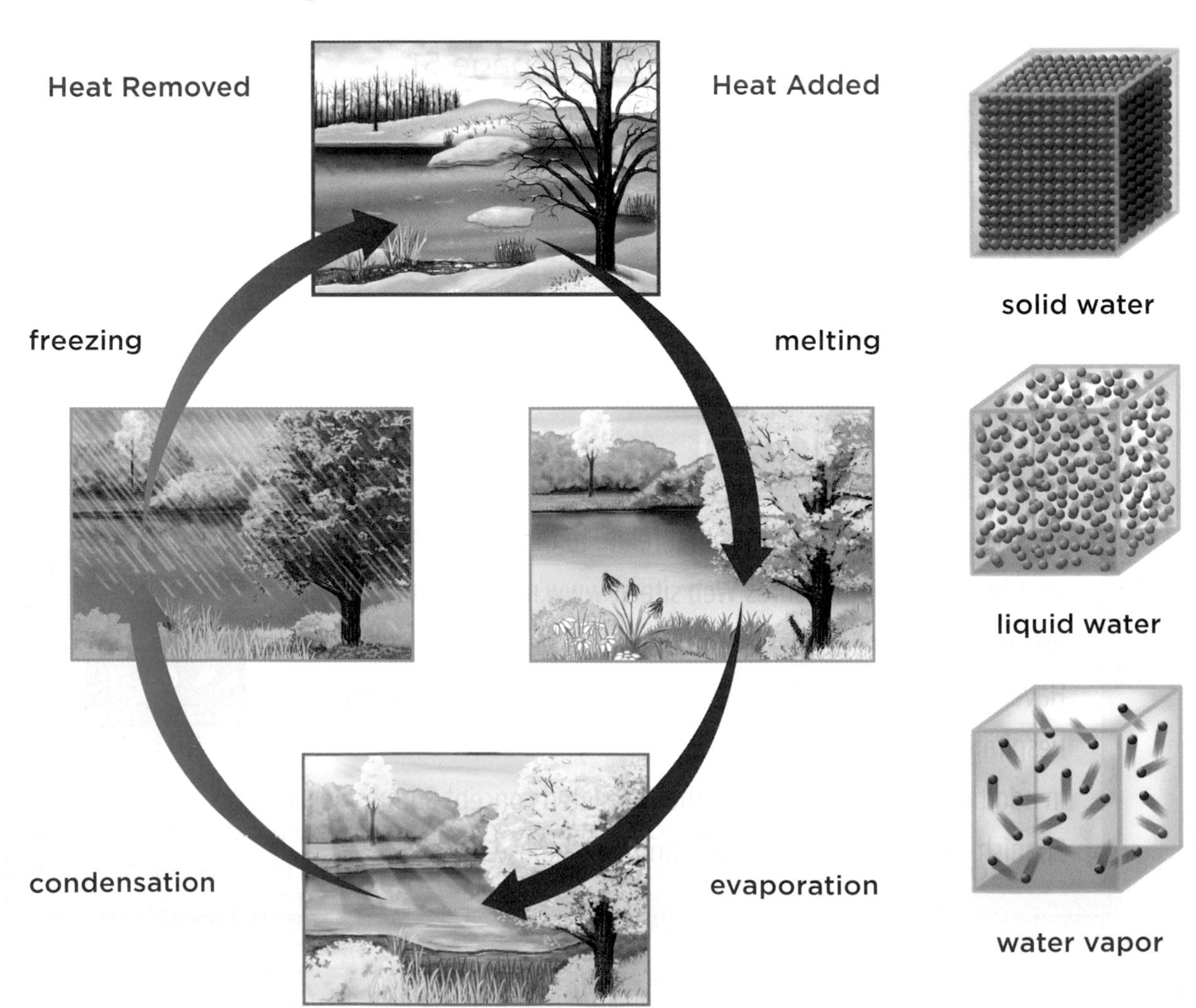

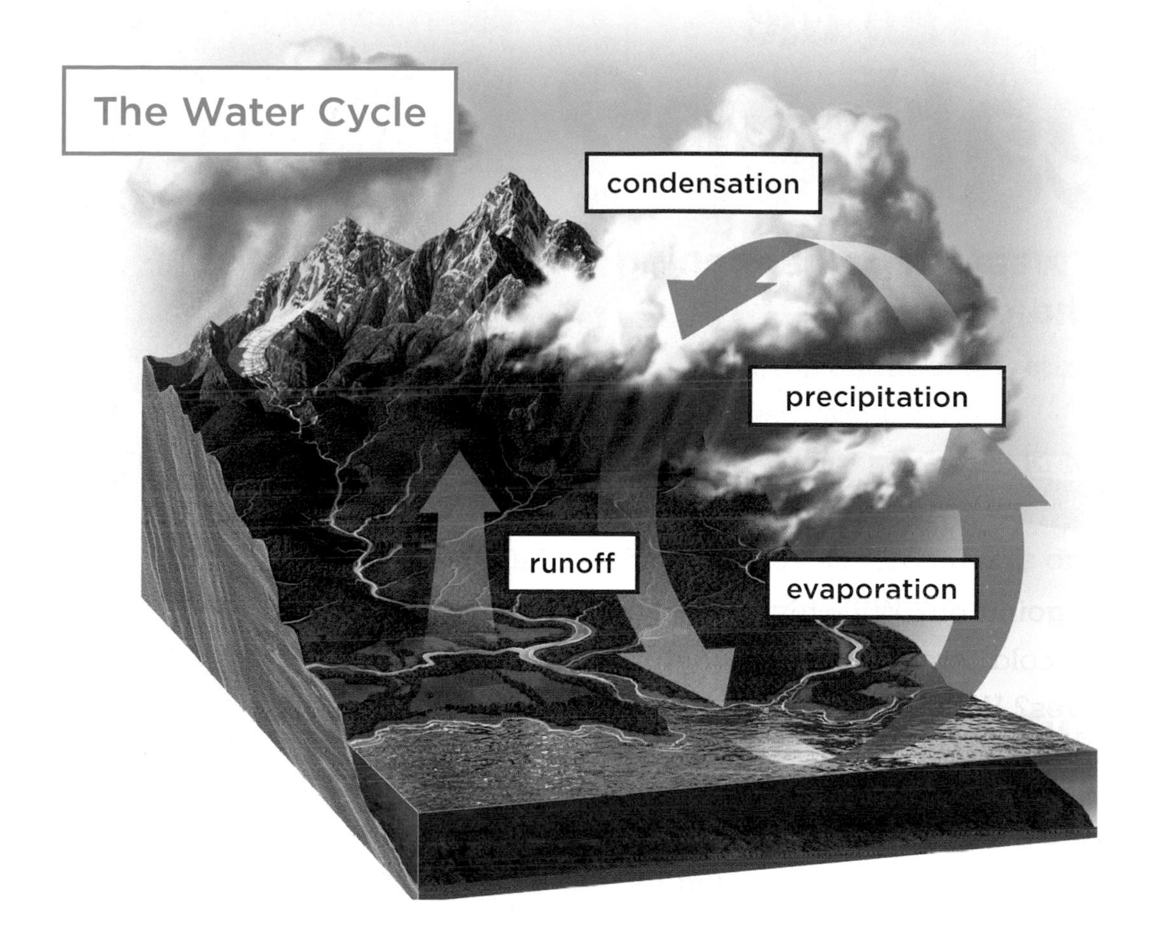

As spring turns to summer, the air becomes hotter. The heat makes liquid water turn into gas, or evaporate. The water in the pond becomes shallow, or less deep. As summer turns to fall, cooler temperatures cause water vapor to change into liquid water. The process of water vapor changing to liquid water is called **condensation**.

Water changes from gas to liquid and from liquid to solid when heat is taken away. When heat is added, water changes from solid to liquid and from liquid to gas.

Water on Earth is never lost. It changes form and moves from place to place. This process, called the **water cycle**, is the continuous movement of water between Earth's surface and the air. Water changes state as part of the cycle.

Water vapor from the ocean evaporates and then condenses into clouds. **Fog** is a cloud that forms near the ground. Water falls as **precipitation** in the form of rain, sleet, hail, or snow. Precipitation runs to the ocean, where it evaporates again.

Welcome to the Worst Weather in the World

Climbing Mount Washington can be a thrill or a dangerous encounter with cold and wind.

Mount Washington, in the White Mountains of New Hampshire, isn't the tallest peak in the United States. It isn't even the hardest to climb. You don't even have to climb it. You can drive up or ride a cog railway to the top.

Mount Washington is famous, though, for having the world's worst weather. Storms blow up without warning. Hikers can die of the cold, even in summer.

The mountain holds the world record for wind speed. In 1934, wind on the mountain blew 231 miles per hour—faster than the strongest hurricane!

It may sound surprising that a not-very-tall (6,288 feet) mountain in New Hampshire has such terrible weather. How can it be colder than the North Pole, windier than the South Pole, and stormier than Tornado Alley?

Snow-covered Mount Washington looms over this New Hampshire hotel.

Charles Krebs/Corbis

Christopher Morris/Corbis

▲ Ice and snow cover the Mount Washington Observatory.

In the Path of the Storms

Winds usually blow storms from west to east across the United States.

When storms reach New Hampshire, they hit the White Mountains, a mountain range that stretches more or less north to south. The winds hit the mountains, then stream upward. The winds speed up.

The fast winds squeeze between the mountains. The fierce winds blast. The shape of the mountain range guides the winds toward Mount Washington. A calm day up here is very rare.

Studying the Weather Where It Lives

Scientists at the Mount Washington Observatory study the natural systems that cause Earth's weather and climate. They conduct weather research, run educational programs, and study cosmic rays.

Members who pay to be part of the observatory can take part in weather research. They can also come up to the top of the mountain for special programs. *—Lisa Jo Rudy*

Mount Washington Extremes

- Coldest winter day on Mount Washington: –120°F. That is as cold as Antarctica!
- Winter snowfall can reach 566 inches. Even in May, 100 inches of snow is not unusual.
- Rime ice often covers buildings at the top of the mountain. These sideways icicles form when supercooled fog hits and freezes on contact.
- Over 100 people have died on the mountain, mostly of the cold. Others have died in avalanches or from drowning.

Around the World in 20 Days

In 1999 two men landed their hot-air balloon in the Egyptian desert and made history.

Fabrice Coffrini/AP Photo

Brian Jones and Bertrand Piccard

Fabrice Coffrini/AP Photo

From Switzerland...

...to Egypt

AP Photo

In March 1999, Bertrand Piccard of Switzerland and Brian Jones of Britain circled the world. They traveled 29,056 miles in a hot-air balloon called the *Breitling Orbiter 3*.

Piccard and Jones were the first to go around the world in a balloon. Weather experts, technology, good luck, and good winds helped them.

How do hot-air balloons fly? When air in a balloon is heated, it becomes less dense—it expands (spreads out). When it is heated enough, the balloon can float. Hot-air balloons have to be big. To lift 1,000 pounds, you need about 65,000 cubic feet of hot air. Piccard and Jones didn't depend on hot air alone. They also used helium, a light gas that is used to make party balloons float.

Inside the *Breitling Orbiter 3*

Piccard and Jones built a cabin below the balloon. Inside they had equipment. There was a basic stove, a heater, a toilet, and plenty of freeze-dried food. As the balloon flew, the heater broke. Other equipment also stopped working. Jones said that "although we did have some great views, we had to scrape off the ice before we could see outside."

Making It Around the World

No one can steer a hot-air balloon. Instead, you have to catch the wind going in the direction you want to go. Piccard and Jones did this by riding jet streams. Jet streams are fast-moving winds that blow high above the ground, usually from west to east.

The annual balloon festival at Chateau-d'Oex

Piccard and Jones took off from Chateau-d'Oex in the Swiss Alps on March 1, 1999. They landed in the Sahara Desert in Egypt after traveling all the way around the world.

Bad weather would have ended the expedition. "We were incredibly lucky with the weather—there were storms chasing us over China, for example, but they never caught us," Jones says.

After the Flight

After their historic flight, Piccard and Jones started a company to encourage other balloonists. They started a tournament with competitions for balloonists. In 2006, the competition changed. It became an international ballooning festival at Chateau-d'Oex. For one week, thousands of hot-air balloons took flight.

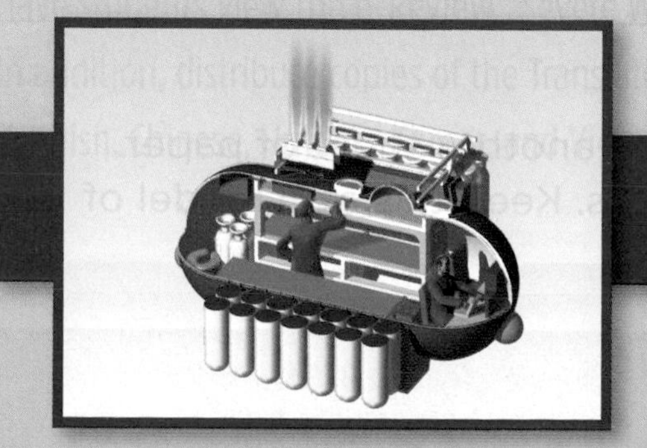

This diagram shows the inside of the balloon's cabin.

Looks Like Earth

Astronomers are very interested in a planet that could support life—and it's only 120 trillion miles away.

JPL/California Institute of Technology/NASA

Is there life on other planets? To find out, astronomers study stars and their movements. If a star moves irregularly at a certain point, there is likely a planet nearby, causing this movement.

There are lots of planets like Jupiter, but not many at all like Earth.

Planet Hunters

Astronomers found evidence of many planets, but none of these could support life. The planets are like Jupiter, which has too much gravity, no water, and no firm surfaces to stand on. Over the past few years, 230 more planets have been discovered. Could any of them support life?

Finally, in 2007, astronomers announced that they had discovered Gliese 581c, a planet outside the solar system that might support life. "It's a significant step on the way to finding possible life in the universe," says Michel Mayor, one of the astronomers who discovered the planet.

Martin Bernetti/AFP/Getty Images

The planet Gliese 581c was first spotted by astronomers at the European Southern Observatory in Chile.

(tr) European Space Observatory/AP Photo (cr) European Space Observatory/AP Photo

Introducing Gliese 581c

Gliese 581c has temperatures like ours on Earth. The star it orbits is much smaller than the Sun.

The mass of Gliese 581c is about five times greater than Earth's mass. This makes its gravity much stronger. Walking on Gliese 581c would probably be impossible.

Astronomers do not yet know if there is liquid water on Gliese 581c. "Liquid water is critical to life as we know it," says Xavier Delfosse, an astronomer on the discovery team.

The planet orbits a red dwarf star (inset).

Right in Our Own Cosmic Backyard

Gliese 581c is 120 trillion miles from Earth, in the constellation Libra. It would take 20 years to get there, travelling at the speed of light. "This planet will most probably be a very important target of the future space missions dedicated to the search for extraterrestrial life," Delfosse says. *—Lisa Jo Rudy*

AFP/Getty Images

The universe may have other planets that support life.

A VARIED LAND

Over thousands of years, many Native American groups lived in North America in different climates and landscapes. Each group had its own culture.

The Arctic is one of Earth's harshest environments. Yet the Inuit have lived there for more than 2,000 years. They settled in the land that is now northern and northwestern Alaska, Canada, and Greenland. The Inuit also live in Siberia in Russia.

Arctic winters are dark and cold, but summers are sunny and mild. The Inuit have adjusted to changing seasons. In the winter, Inuit men built houses out of soil and wood. They built parts of the houses underground. When they traveled to hunt, men built igloo homes made of large snow blocks. In the warmer weather, they used wooden poles and animal skins to make tents.

The Inuit hunted animals such as walruses, seals, fish, and whales. These animals provided meat, skins, and materials for making weapons and tools. Their fat was burned, providing heat and light.

Life was different in other places, such as the forests east of the Mississippi River. Groups who lived there had all the trees, plants, and animals they needed.

In the 1500s the Iroquois lived mostly in what is now upstate New York. Historians call this group Iroquois because of the Iroquoian languages the people spoke. However, the Iroquois call themselves Hodenosaunee. In Iroquoian this means "people of the longhouse." **Longhouses** are long buildings made of poles covered with sheets of bark.

Iroquois men built houses, hunted, fished, and were responsible for fighting. Iroquois women gathered food. They also cooked and took care of their homes. Iroquois women also decided how the land would be used and who would use it. They were the leaders of their clans. A **clan** is a group of families who share the same ancestor. The clan leader chose the village leaders. She approved all clan decisions.

Clans controlled most property. Women owned the land and the longhouses. Married couples lived in the wife's longhouse. Her family lived there. Children shared the mother's clan name.

In about 1570, five Iroquois groups formed the **Iroquois Confederacy**. The goal was to keep the peace between the Iroquois nations.

The Iroquois set up the Great Law, rules that the people followed. The Grand Council, made up of people from each nation, worked together to make decisions. Members learned to use compromise. In a **compromise**, people or groups give up some things so that everyone can get some, but not all, of what they want.

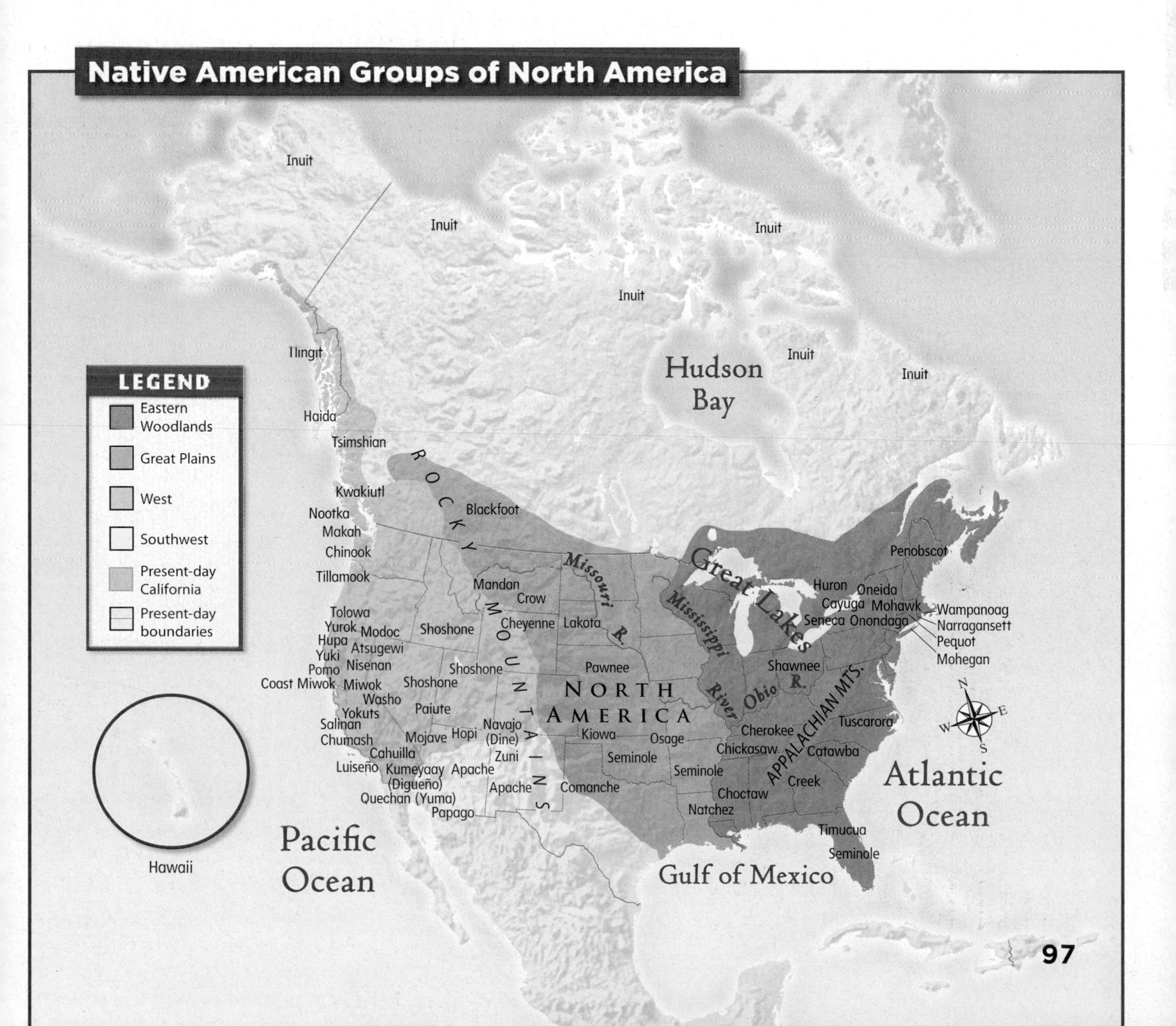

Who Were the First Americans?

An ancient skeleton gives us clues.

For a long time, scientists had one idea about how the first people got to the Americas. They believed that 12,000 years ago, people walked on dry land from what is now Russia to Alaska. Now, scientists are not so sure.

Kennewick Man

In 1996 two college students were digging on the bank of the Columbia River, near Kennewick, Washington. They found a skull that looked ancient. More bones were found later. Tests showed that the skeleton was 9,400 years old!

The skeleton was called Kennewick Man. It is one of the oldest complete skeletons ever found in the Americas.

Kennewick Man

A scientist examines the skull of Kennewick man. ▶

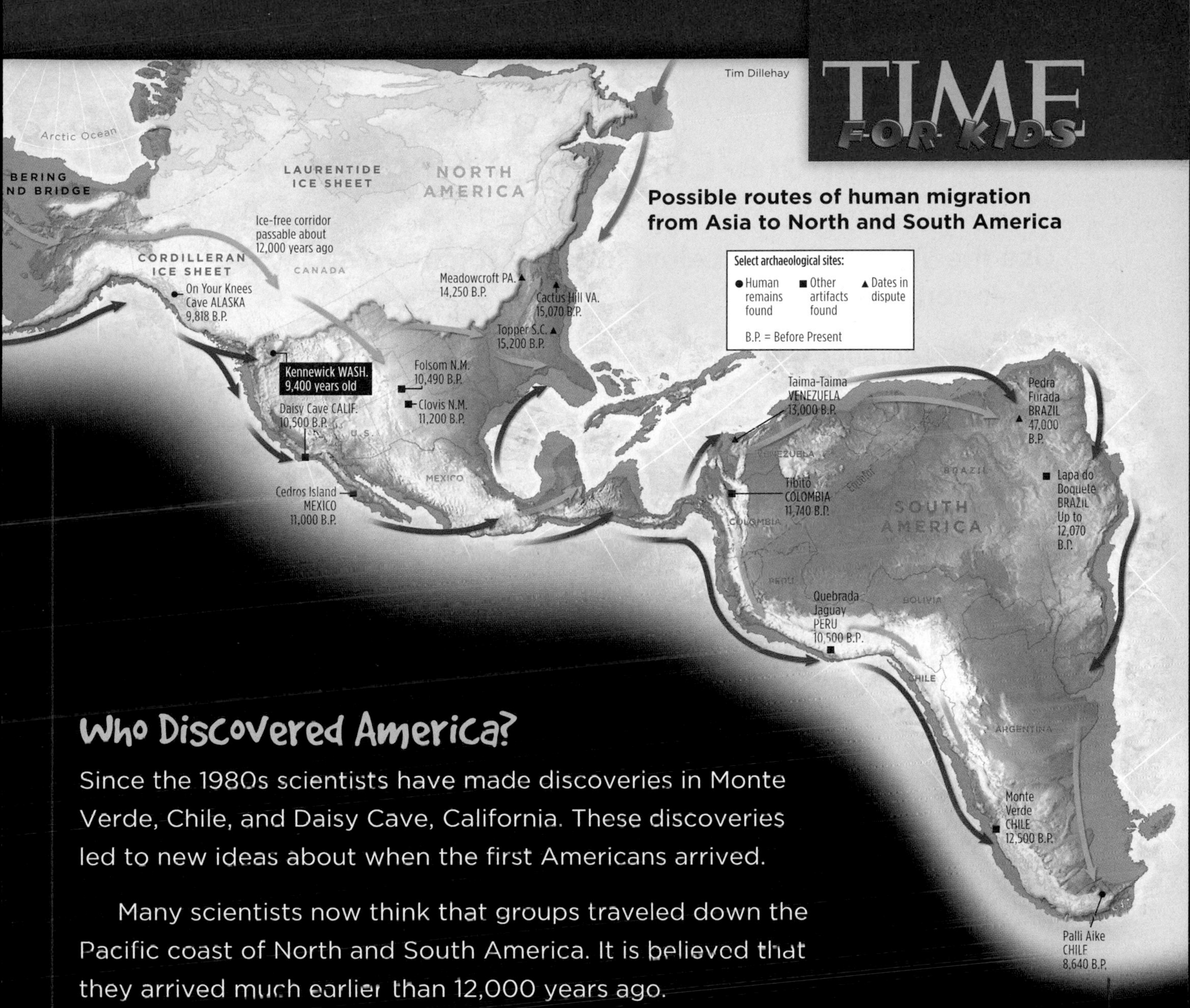

Who Discovered America?

Since the 1980s scientists have made discoveries in Monte Verde, Chile, and Daisy Cave, California. These discoveries led to new ideas about when the first Americans arrived.

Many scientists now think that groups traveled down the Pacific coast of North and South America. It is believed that they arrived much earlier than 12,000 years ago.

Scientists have also made discoveries in South Carolina. A few believe that early Americans may have come from Europe to the Atlantic Coast. *—Michael D. Lemonick and Andrea Dorfman*

An artist's drawing of what Kennewick Man might have looked like ▶

Raul Colon

Something to Think About

Who should own ancient bones, scientists or the people who own the land where they were found? Why?

Compare/Contrast Writing Frame

Use the Writing Frame below to orally summarize "A Varied Land."

When you **compare** the Inuit and Iroquois, you discover that

they **both** used ______________________________.

The Inuit settled in the land that is today ______________________

______________________________.

In contrast, the Iroquois lived ______________________

______________________________.

Like Iroquois men, Inuit men ______________________________.

Inuit and Iroquois homes were **different** because ______________________

______________________________.

Inuit and Iroquois women performed tasks such as ______________________

______________________________.

Unlike the Inuit women, Iroquois women decided ______________________

______________________________.

Use the frame to write the summary on another sheet of paper. Be sure to include the **bold** signal words. Keep this as a model of this Text Structure.

Critical Thinking

1. A building made of poles covered with sheets of bark is called a ________________.

   A. longhouse

   B. clan

   C. igloo

2. Find the sentence in "A Varied Land" that explains what *compromise* means.

3. Find the paragraph in "Who Were the First Americans?" that tells when and where Kennewick Man was found.

4. Study the map on page 99. With a partner, discuss how early people could have traveled from place to place.

The legend or key on a map helps you understand what symbols or colors mean.

Digital Learning

For a list of links and activities that relate to this History/Social Science standard, visit the California Treasures Web site at www.macmillanmh.com to access the Content Readers resources. Have students view "Native People of North America."

TRADE AND TRAVEL

About 1,500 years ago, Europe was made up of small countries. They were often at war with one another. This period of European history, called the **Middle Ages**, occurred long before the start of modern cultures like our own.

During the Middle Ages, people learned more about science, medicine, and technology. Merchants learned about these ideas as they traveled around, buying and selling goods. Back home, they told others what they had learned.

During the Middle Ages, people of different religions often fought. From 1095 to 1270, European Christians and Muslims fought for control of the Holy Land. This was known as the **Crusades**. During the 1400s, Spanish Christians recaptured their lands from Moors, Arab followers of the religion of Islam. This event is called **Reconquista**.

In 1517 a German priest named Martin Luther wanted to reform, or make changes to, the Roman Catholic Church. He and his followers became known as Protestant Christians because they protested against the Church. Their actions are called the **Protestant Reformation**. Catholic leaders met to solve their problems. Their efforts are called the **Counter Reformation**.

▼ **Martin Luther preaches to a group of German Protestants.**

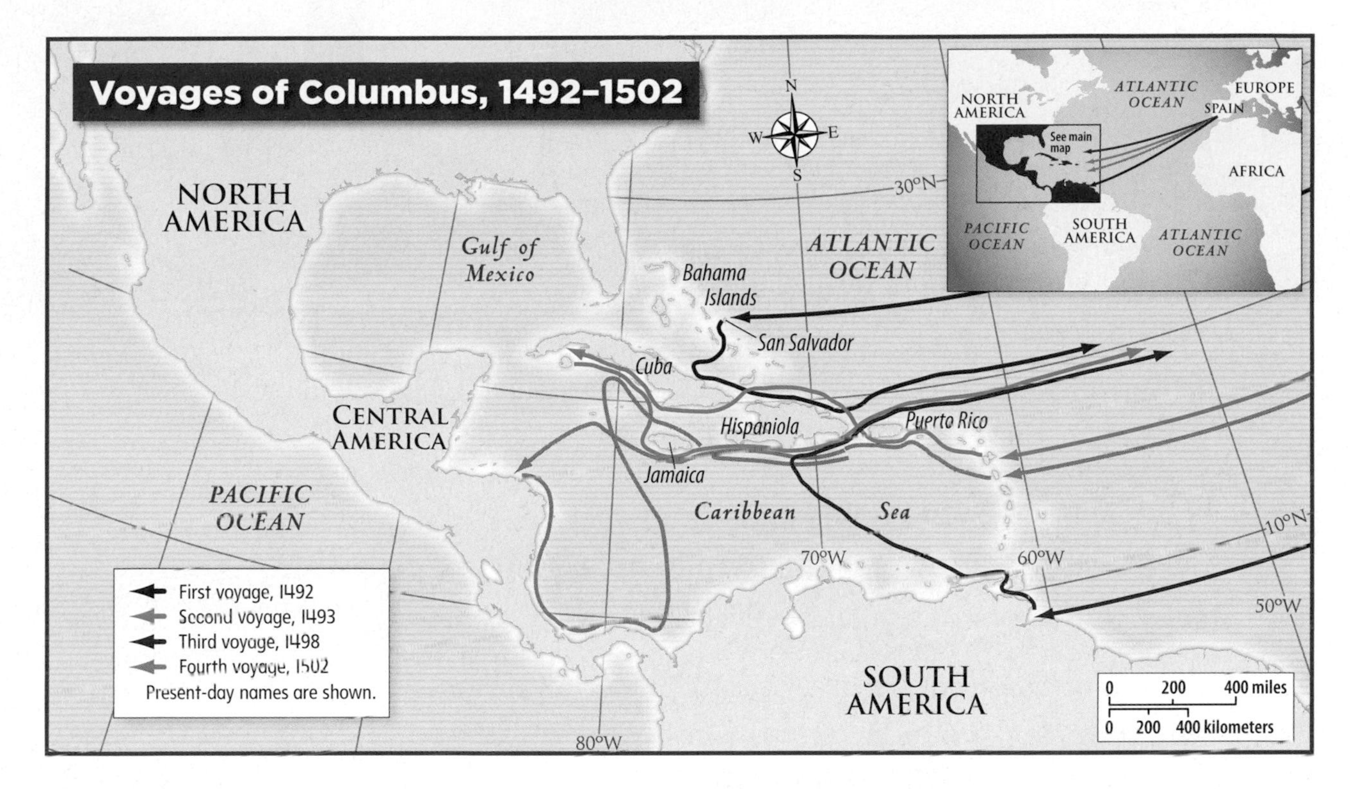

Europeans became explorers. By the late 1400s, Europeans wanted to explore the islands of Southeast Asia. They called the islands the Indies. They knew the Indies held great riches, including spices, silk, and gold. Portuguese and Mediterranean traders controlled the sea routes around Africa to Asia. The Portuguese were the best sailors. In the early 1400s, Portugal's Prince Henry had asked experts to study **navigation**, or using maps and compasses to find and follow the best sea routes.

Other Europeans believed reaching the Indies would bring them fortune. Christopher Columbus, a sailor from Genoa, Italy, wanted to sail west from Europe. He believed this would be the fastest route. Queen Isabella and King Ferdinand of Spain agreed to pay for his **expedition**. An expedition is a journey made for a special purpose.

After months at sea, Columbus reached the Bahamas Islands on October 12, 1492. He thought he was in the Indies. He called the local people *Indios*, which is Spanish for "Indians." They were actually part of a Native American group called the Taíno.

Columbus traveled three more times to the Americas. On his third voyage, he reached South America. His expeditions encouraged other brave explorers.

Explorers and Technology

Gary C. Knapp/AP Photo

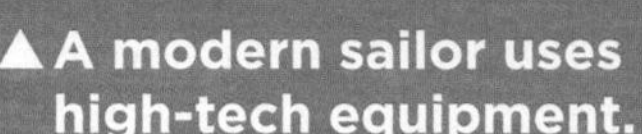

▲ A modern sailor uses high-tech equipment.

Datacraft/Getty Images

The ocean is a huge place. Today's sailors use global positioning systems, cell phones, satellite phones, and radios to be sure they're headed in the right direction.

How did explorers like Christopher Columbus, Francisco Vásquez de Coronado, James Cook, and Ferdinand Magellan know where they were and where to go?

They used the stars to guide them. They used mechanics and the laws of physics, too. *—Lisa Jo Rudy*

Columbus used the stars to help find his way to the New World.

Bettmann/Corbis

Josh Westrich/zefa/Corbis

The Astrolabe

The North Star (Polaris) can help sailors find their location. To see Polaris, though, the sky must be clear. Polaris cannot be seen in some places.

The astrolabe was the first navigation tool. It helped sailors find locations using the Sun, Moon, planets, and stars. Users had to know math and astronomy.

Werner Forman/Corbis

The Compass

A compass has a magnetic needle that always points north. This can be seen on a circle that is marked north, south, east, and west. Before compasses, sailors used stars to find direction.

No one knows who invented the compass. It may have come from South America, Central America, or ancient China.

The Granger Collection

The Sextant

Another navigation tool is the sextant. It measures the angle between the horizon and an object like the Sun or Moon.

The first sextant was made in 994 in Iran. In time, it became more popular than the astrolabe. Sailors use it to this day.

The Granger Collection

Description Writing Frame

Use the Writing Frame below to orally summarize "Explorers and Technology."

Before today's technology, sailors used other **tools** to help them sail across the ocean.

One important tool was the astrolabe. It is a tool that helps find

____

____.

To use one, you need to know ______________________

____.

The compass is **another important tool**. A compass always ________

____.

The sextant was another important tool. Sailors used it to ________

____.

Because of these important tools, explorers were able to travel all over the world!

Use the frame to write the summary on another sheet of paper. Be sure to include the **bold** signal words. Keep this as a model of this Text Structure.

Critical Thinking

1 A journey made for a special purpose is called a ________________.

A. crusade

B. navigation

C. expedition

2 Find the paragraph in "Explorers and Technology" that tells what a compass is.

3 Point to the paragraph in "Trade and Travel" that explains the Protestant Reformation.

4 With your finger, trace the four voyages of Columbus that are shown on the map on page 103. Compare and contrast the voyages.

The information in map keys helps readers understand what a map shows.

Digital Learning

For a list of links and activities that relate to this History/Social Science standard, visit the California Treasures Web site at www.macmillanmh.com to access the Content Readers resources. Have students view "Exploration and Colonization."

EXPLORING THE AMERICAS

In the 1500s, Spain had colonies in Central America and the Caribbean. From here, Spanish explorers traveled north to the **frontier**, the area at the edge of a settled place. At the time, the frontier was the land that would later become the United States. The first person to explore this land was Juan Ponce de León, who reached Florida's Gulf Coast in 1513.

In 1528, a hurricane shipwrecked a Spanish crew led by Alvar Nuñez Cabeza de Vaca onto the coast of what is now Texas. The men lived among Native Americans in Texas for four years. Then they walked to Mexico. They arrived in Mexico City in 1536.

In 1538 Hernado de Soto and his army began an expedition. Seeking riches, they traveled nearly 4,000 miles across what is now the southeastern United States. They were the first Europeans to see the Mississippi River. De Soto became ill and died in 1542. He never found a treasure.

In 1542 Portuguese explorer Juan Rodríguez Cabrillo led the first European expedition to what is now California. Sixty years later, Sebastian Vizcaíno claimed California land for Spain. The names he gave to places are still used today.

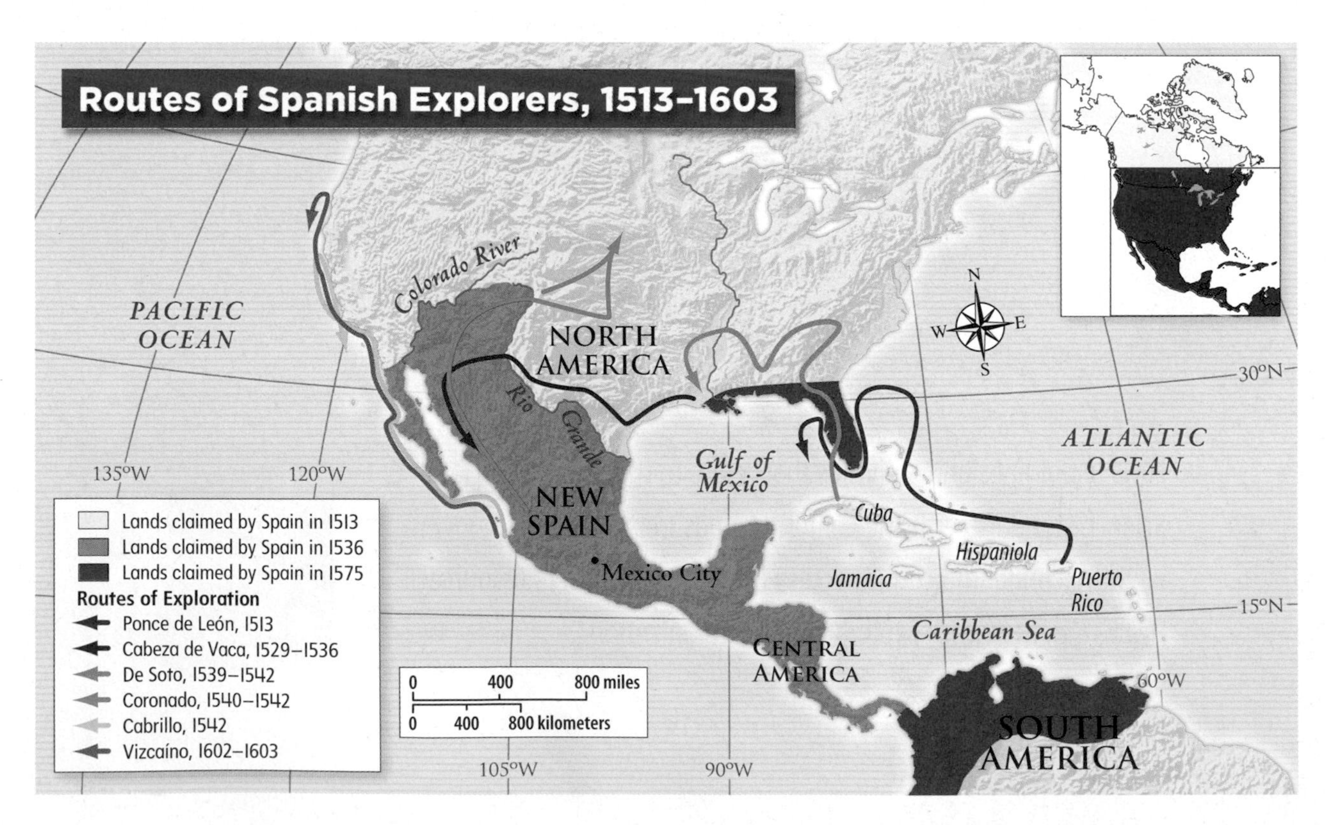

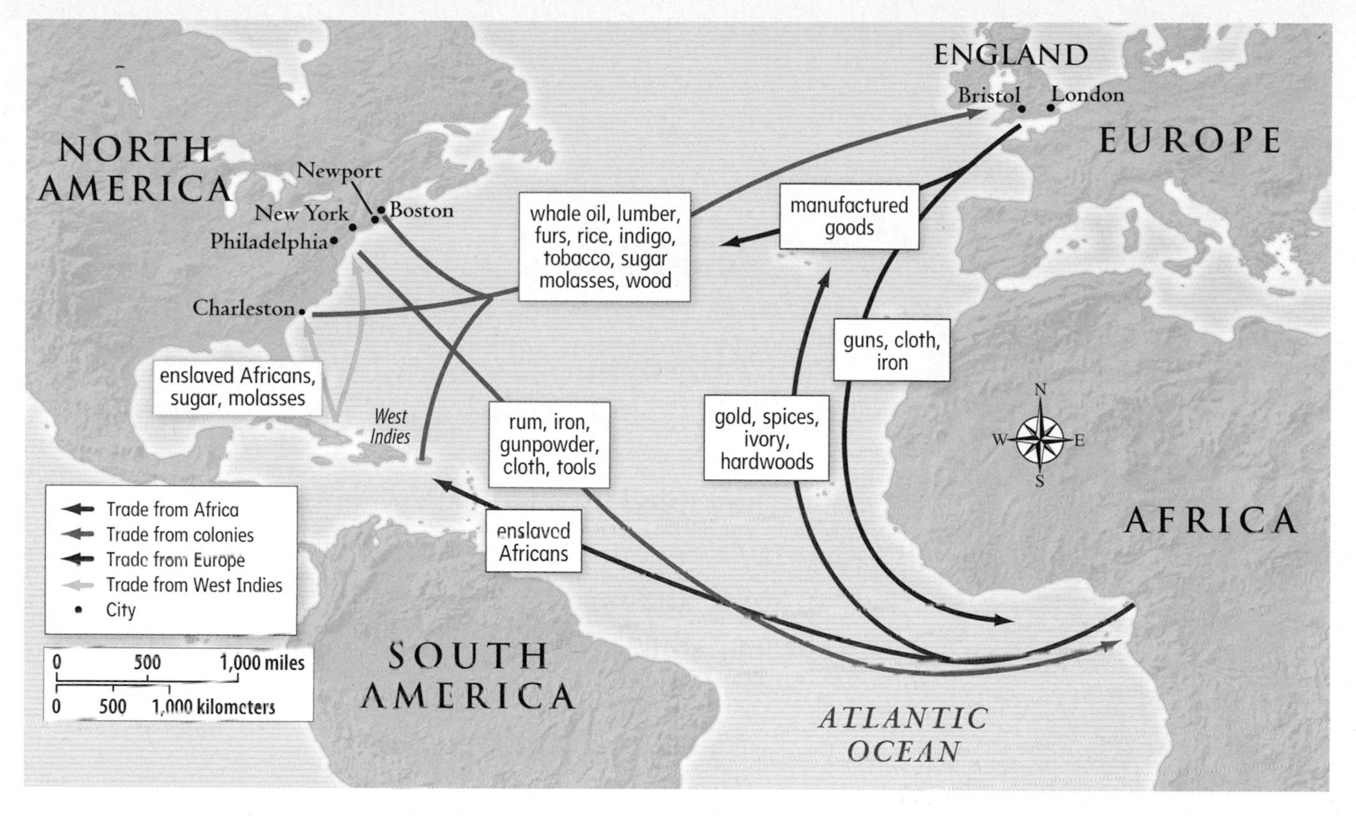

▲ **Triangular trade carried goods and people to four continents.**

In the meantime, other Europeans searched for a shortcut to Asia. This was a water route, now called the **Northwest Passage**. It was believed to connect the Atlantic and Pacific Oceans.

The English, French, and Dutch hired explorers such as John Cabot, Giovanni de Verrazano, and Henry Hudson to search for this route. They did not find the Northwest Passage, but their expeditions helped start New France, New Netherlands, New Sweden, and the English colonies.

Ships that sailed between England, Africa, and the West Indies took part in **triangular trade**. By the late 1600s, English colonies in North America started their own triangular trade with Africa and the West Indies. Triangular trade was designed to sell products and pick up cargo at each stop.

Three voyages were needed. On the first of the three voyages, traders sailed from New England to Africa. They brought manufactured goods, including guns, gunpowder, rum, and cloth. These goods were traded for African captives.

On the second of the voyages, the traders took the African captives to the West Indies. In the West Indies, the Africans were sold into slavery. There the ships picked up molasses, a thick syrup made from sugarcane.

The third voyage went from the West Indies back to North America. North Americans bought the molasses. They used it to make rum. Then the trade began again.

The *Taíno* greet Columbus in what is now called Cuba.

Taíno art on the wall of a cave in the Dominican Republic

The Taíno World: Contact and Impact

The Taíno almost vanished after European explorers and settlers arrived.

They lived on islands throughout the Caribbean. They were traders, fishermen, hunters, and farmers. They made many types of tools, musical instruments, and pottery. Then millions of them died after meeting European explorers. They were the Taíno.

A Vanished Way of Life

In 1492 the Taíno lived in island countries we now call Cuba, Puerto Rico, Jamaica, the Bahamas, Haiti, and the Dominican Republic.

Taíno farmers grew pineapple, guava, and papaya. They also grew squash, beans, peppers, tobacco, and cotton. The Taíno built huge canoes for fishing and long-distance trading. Some of the canoes could hold 100 people. They also made wooden spears and household items.

▼A Taíno stool

Do You Speak Arawak?

These words come from the Taíno's language, Arawak:

hurricane barbecue hammock canoe

The End of a World

Some Taíno communities had thousands of people. Then Columbus and the early Spanish explorers arrived.

The explorers carried diseases that were fatal to the people they met. Those who didn't die of disease were enslaved or killed. The explorers took Taíno land and possessions.

The Beginning of Sugar

In the Caribbean islands, Europeans grew crops like coffee and bananas. These crops had never been grown on Caribbean islands before. African slaves did the work.

Then the Dutch started growing sugarcane, a very valuable crop. It gives us sugar. The British built sugar plantations on Jamaica, Barbados, and other smaller islands. These plantations became the British Empire's most valuable possessions. *—Susan Moger*

The Taíno Today

Thousands of Taíno descendants are alive and well. They live in Cuba, the Dominican Republic, Haiti, and the United States. Some even live in Spain.

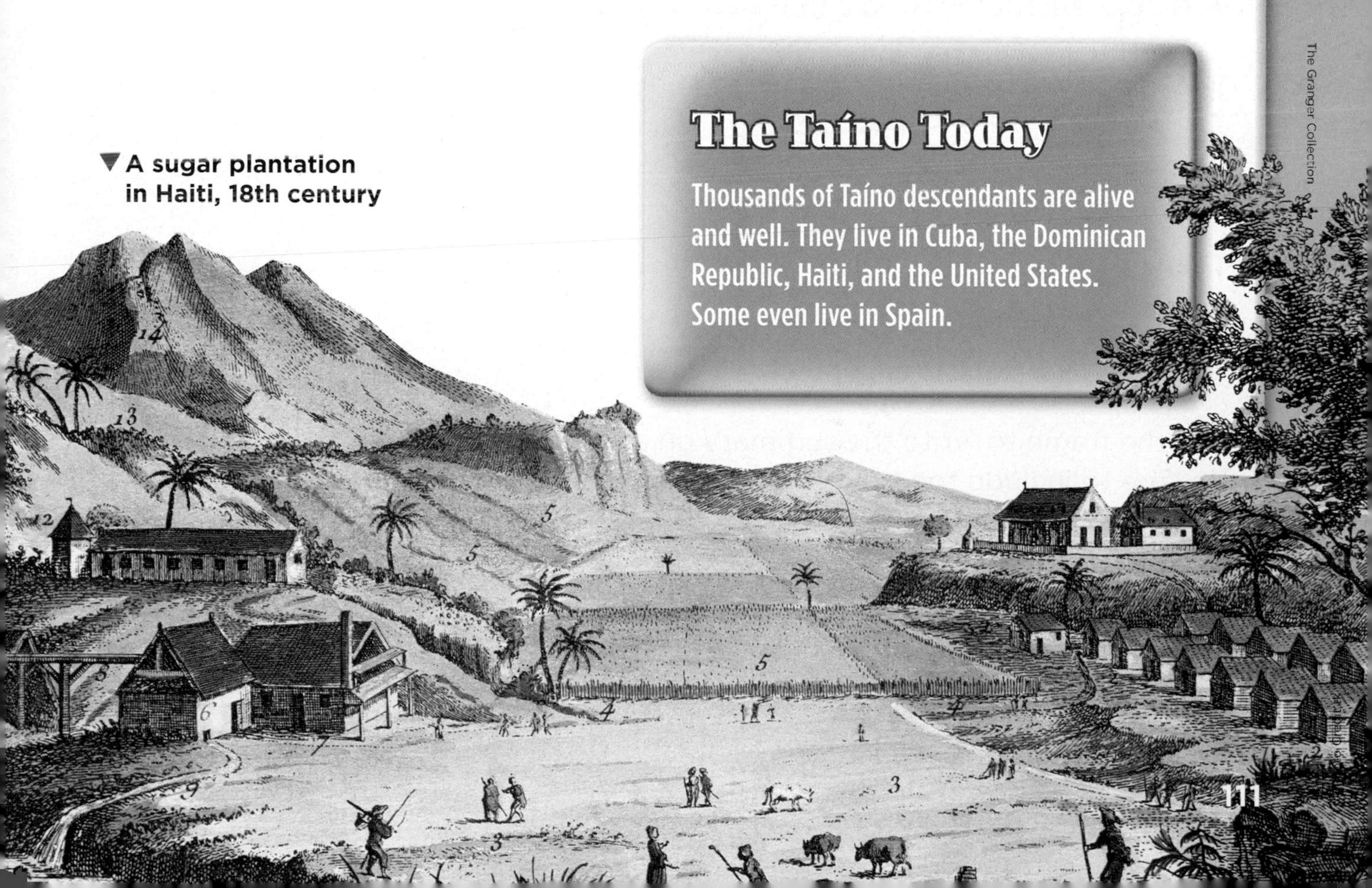

▼ A sugar plantation in Haiti, 18th century

Sequence Writing Frame

Use the Writing Frame below to orally summarize "Exploring the Americas."

In the 1500s Spanish explorers entered frontier land that would later become the United States.

In 1528 Cabeza de Vaca was shipwrecked onto ______________________________

____.

For the next four years, he and his men ______________________________

____.

In 1536 Cabeza de Vaca's group walked to ______________________________.

In 1538, Hernado de Soto and his army wanted to find ____________________.

They became the first Europeans to ______________________________

____.

Then in 1542, Juan Rodríguez Cabrillo ______________________________

____.

Use the frame to write the summary on another sheet of paper. Be sure to include the **bold** signal words. Keep this as a model of this Text Structure.

Critical Thinking

1 The routes between Africa, the West Indies, and colonial New England are called ________________.

A. the Middle Passage

B. the Northwest Passage

C. triangular trade

2 Point to the place in "Exploring the United States" that describes what *frontier* means.

3 Locate the paragraph in "The Taíno World: Contact and Impact" that explains what the British Empire's most valuable possession was.

4 Review the map "Routes of Spanish Explorers, 1513-1603" on page 108. About how close is Cuba to New Spain? Share your ideas with a partner.

A scale shows the relationship between distances on a map and real distances.

Digital Learning

For a list of links and activities that relate to this History/Social Science standard, visit the California Treasures Web site at www.macmillanmh.com to access the Content Readers resources. Have students read "St. Augustine, Florida."

THE FRENCH AND INDIAN WAR

By the 1700s, England, France, and Spain took control of lands in North America. This land was home to many Native Americans.

Some lands were claimed by both France and England. Disagreements over who could live there led to a conflict called the **French and Indian War**. The English (also known as the British) fought the French and their Native American friends, the Wyandot.

For the first half of the 1700s, Native Americans controlled the Ohio River Valley. Some of them sold their lands to colonists. France began to build forts on the new lands to stop the British from taking the lands. The British decided to drive the French out.

The lieutenant governor of Virginia, Robert Dinwiddie, sent young George Washington to lead British troops to Fort Duquesne (present-day Pittsburgh). On May 28, 1754, Washington's troops defeated the French.

On July 3, 1754, the French and Native Americans attacked the British. The British were defeated. Washington and his men returned to Virginia.

Along with the Wyandot, other Native American groups helped the French. They taught the French to hide behind trees and large rocks and to attack the British who marched into open spaces.

News of French victories frightened British colonists. They feared the French would kill them or force them out of North America. The colonists begged British leader William Pitt for help. He agreed. With more troops and equipment, the British began to win.

British soldiers in the French and Indian War

In June 1759, British forces attacked Quebec. After three months of fighting, the French surrendered Quebec on September 13. A year later, British general Amherst seized Montreal. With this victory, England (now called Great Britain) controlled Canada.

Eventually, France lost the war. In 1763, France and Great Britain signed the **Treaty of Paris**, which ended the French and Indian War. Britain gained control of former French lands east of the Mississippi River.

When the war ended, Great Britain told colonists where they could and could not live. For them, a smaller area required less protection. To stop British settlements in the Ohio River Valley, Great Britain issued the **Proclamation of 1763**. This proclamation, or official announcement, set aside all British land west of the Appalachians for Native Americans.

Many colonists disobeyed the proclamation, moving to lands west of the Appalachians. Colonists soon realized they could not count on their country of origin to protect them from Native American attacks.

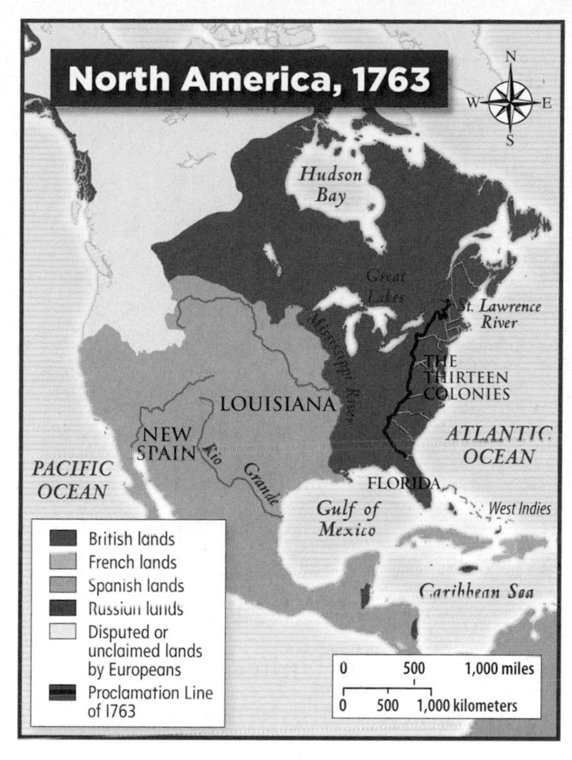

Colonists did, however, feel united and strong. They had taken part in the French and Indian War, and had been on the winning side. Their leaders could bring people together.

Soon the colonies would come together. Together, they would fight Great Britain for their own independence.

The French and Indian War

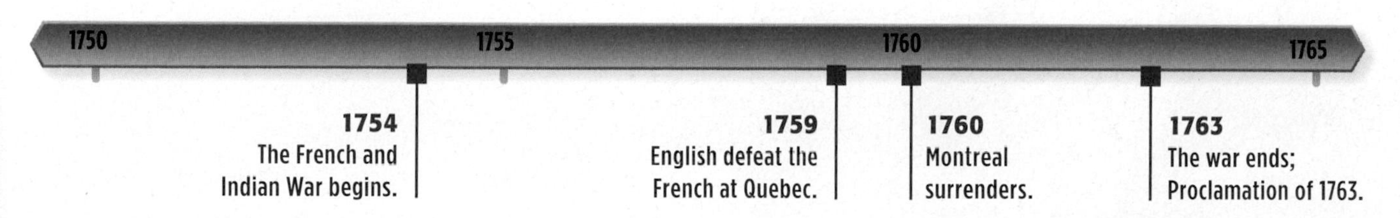

The Bridgeman Art Library

English ships arrive in Jamestown

Jamestown:

Competition, Conflict, and Cooperation

The first English colony in the Americas had a difficult start.

A Business Proposition

Jamestown was the first English colony in what is now the United States. The 104 English colonists who arrived in 1607 hoped to collect treasures for England.

The London Company paid for the trip, hoping for a profit. However, the colonists settled on swampy land. They did not know how to grow food there.

Trade or No Trade

The colonists wanted to trade with the Powhatan who lived in the area. The colonists needed food, but the Powhatan would not trade with them during the winter of 1609–1610. Most of the colonists starved. By the spring, only 60 of 500 colonists were left alive.

Relations with Indians: War

As more colonists arrived, they started farms—as if to stay for good. This angered the Powhatan. In 1622 they attacked settlements along the James River, killing 347 colonists. Jamestown was saved because a Native American boy had warned the colonists.

Burgandy Beam

Association for the Preservation of Virginia Antiquities

▲ A model of the Jamestown settlement

The colonists fought back in July 1624. In two days, 60 well-armed colonists defeated 800 Native Americans.

From Tobacco . . .

The Jamestown colonists found "gold" in growing tobacco. Indentured servants and African slaves did the work. Indentured servants had to work for seven years. Then they were free. Slaves had to work their whole lives.

. . . to Representative Government

In 1618 property owners elected the first general assembly of burgesses (representatives). The assembly's job was to advise the governor. From this seed grew Virginia's House of Burgesses. That's where George Washington and Thomas Jefferson got their start.

America's Birthplace

The history of Jamestown includes greed, war, and death, but also bravery and the beginning of representative government. *—Adapted from TIME*

John Smith Visits the Chief

John Smith was a leader of Jamestown colony. He described his visit to Powhatan chief Wahunsonacock in December 1607: "He sat covered with a great robe, made of raccoon skins . . ." Around him were "two rows of men and behind them as many women, with all their heads and shoulders painted red."

Stock Montage/Getty Images

Problem/Solution Writing Frame

Use the Writing Frame below to orally summarize "Jamestown: Competition, Conflict, and Cooperation."

The first English colony in the Americas had a difficult start.

This **problem occurred** because the land was ____________________.

The colonists could not ____________________.

One solution was to ____________________.

When the colonists tried this solution ____________________.

As a result, ____________________.

The Powhatan became angry because ____________________

____________________.

The result was ____________________.

Jamestown escaped **because** ____________________

____________________.

In the two-day battle, 60 well-armed colonists fought 800 Native

Americans. **The result** was ____________________

____________________.

Use the frame to write the summary on another sheet of paper.
Be sure to include the **bold** signal words. Keep this as a model of
this Text Structure.

Critical Thinking

1 The French and Indian War was a conflict between ________________.

A. English and French

B. French and Indian

C. Indian and English

2 Find the meaning of *indentured servant* in "Jamestown: Competition, Conflict, and Cooperation."

3 Was the Proclamation of 1763 a success? Locate the paragraph in "The French and Indian War" that helps you form an answer.

4 Review the time line on page 115. Talk to a partner about the length of the French and Indian War.

A time line highlights key events that happened during a certain time period.

Digital Learning

For a list of links and activities that relate to this History/Social Science standard, visit the California Treasures Web site at www.macmillanmh.com to access the Content Readers resources. Have students view "The Struggle for North America."

CONFLICTS IN THE COLONIES

Native Americans lived in lands that became English colonies. They did not want settlers on their land, so conflicts occurred.

When settlers arrived in Jamestown, Virginia, the Powhatan helped them. They were guests in Powhatan villages.

New governor Lord de la Warr arrived in Virginia in 1610. He did not see any colonists. He thought the Powhatan had kidnapped them. He ordered the Powhatan to release them. The chief refused.

The two sides fought. This was the start of the **Powhatan Wars**. Fighting continued for forty years.

The colonists destroyed Powhatan crops and stole their food. Even worse, when the Powhatan met the Europeans, they were exposed to diseases they never had before, such as measles. As many as 90 percent of the Powhatan may have died from diseases that came from Europe.

As the Powhatan population declined, settlers kept coming from England. The Powhatan could no longer keep the settlers off their land. There were 18,000 English settlers in Virginia by 1650.

To the north, Native Americans also feared losing their land to colonists. Conflict between the Pequot and colonists in Plymouth led to the **Pequot War**. The war started in 1636.

The English planned a brutal, surprise attack. They surrounded a wooden Pequot fort and set fire to it. The Pequot were killed or captured as they tried to escape.

Few Pequot survived. Those who escaped the attack were captured and sold into slavery. By 1638 only a few dozen Pequot were still alive. Their lands went to the English. The Pequot went to live with other nearby Native Americans.

After the defeat of the Pequot, English settlers soon lived in areas which are now part of New Hampshire, Vermont, and Maine.

English settlers attacked the Pequot village at Missituck (now Mystic), Connecticut, in the spring of 1637. ▶

▲ Wampanoag attack a farm during King Philip's War.

Another war started when Metacomet became leader of the Wampanoag. He tried to stop the English from taking more land. He sent messengers to his longtime enemies, the Narragansett, for help. They refused, but other Native American groups joined Metacomet.

The brutal war began in 1675. It was called **King Philip's War** because the colonists gave Metacomet the name "King Philip." The war ended in August 1676 when Metacomet was killed by Native Americans who helped the colonists. About 4,000 Native Americans had been killed in the war. Most of the remaining Wampanoag were sold into slavery in the West Indies. Native American power in New England was over.

Another war between settlers and Native Americans started in 1715. At first, the Yamasee helped the British colonists living in the Carolinas. When other Native Americans captured the colonists, the Yamasee rescued them. The Yamasee believed they should be paid in return. However, the colonists did not pay them.

The Yamasee were in debt to British traders. They worried that the traders would enslave them if they could not pay.

The Yamasee decided to attack the colonists. They got weapons from Spanish colonists in Florida. Then the Cherokee joined the fight—on the British side.

In 1717 the Yamasee were defeated. They fled to Florida. The Cherokee then became the most powerful Native Americans in the Carolinas.

The Granger Collection

▲ European settlers meet with Native Americans in what is now Georgia.

Library of Congress, Prints and Photographs Division

▲ Andrew Jackson

The Trail of Tears

President Andrew Jackson forced thousands of Cherokee people to leave their land.

When the first Europeans came to North America, they learned that people were already here. Native Americans lived throughout the continent.

The Indian Removal Act

The people of the Cherokee Nation lived in what is now northern Georgia. Their land had gold. Members of the U.S. government wanted control of that wealth.

In 1830 Congress passed the Indian Removal Act. President Andrew Jackson signed the act. The act said that the Cherokee had to leave their land.

Even the U.S. Supreme Court disagreed with the Act. The justices said the Cherokee Nation was sovereign—that is, it was a country. The Cherokee would have to sign a treaty that said they agreed to leave. The treaty would have to be approved by the U.S. Senate.

In 1835 two Cherokee, Major Ridge and Elias Boudinot, signed the treaty. Most of the Cherokee people did not want to leave their land, but the Senate approved the treaty. It passed by just one vote.

A painting of the Trail of Tears.

Nunna daul Tsuny

In 1838 the U.S. Army forced 17,000 men, women, and children from their land. The Cherokee were forced to march 1,000 miles to Oklahoma. They did not have enough food, blankets, and medicine. More than 4,000 people died along the way. The journey became known as the Trail of Tears or in Cherokee, *Nunna daul Tsuny*.

What Happened Next

The former Cherokee land attracted gold prospectors. Soon they were everywhere. In 1849, however, gold was discovered in California. The prospectors moved on, leaving ghost towns behind.

The Cherokee people continued their traditions in Oklahoma. Today the people of the Cherokee Nation run their own schools and health program. They honor those who suffered and died on the Trail of Tears.

Cherokee traditions are still alive. ▶

Sequence Writing Frame

Use the Writing Frame below to orally summarize "The Trail of Tears."

When the first Europeans came to North America, they learned that people were already here. One of these groups was the Cherokee Nation.

In 1828 the people of the Cherokee Nation lived ______________________________

____.

In 1830, Congress passed ______________________________.

At the same time, the U.S. Supreme Court ______________________________.

The justices said that ______________________________

____.

Then, **in 1835**, ______________________________.

In 1838 ______________________________

____.

The route they traveled became known as ______________________________.

Today, people of the Cherokee Nation still live in Oklahoma.

Use the frame to write the summary on another sheet of paper. Be sure to include the **bold** signal words. Keep this as a model of this Text Structure.

Critical Thinking

1. The 1636 war between Native Americans and the colonists at Plymouth was ________.

   A. the Powhatan War

   B. the Pequot War

   C. King Philip's War

2. Point to the sentences in "Conflicts in the Colonies" that explain why the Yamasee attacked British colonists.

3. Reread the paragraph in "Trail of Tears" that explains the term *sovereign*.

4. Make up a caption for the painting of Andrew Jackson on page 122, and say it aloud.

Captions give the reader additional information about the subject of the article.

Digital Learning

For a list of links and activities that relate to this History/Social Science standard, visit the California Treasures Web site at www.macmillanmh.com to access the Content Readers resources. Have students view "The English Establish 13 Colonies."

WILLIAM PENN FOUNDS A COLONY

In 1651, King Charles II had to leave England. A **revolution**, or change in government, had forced him out. King Charles wanted to return to England in 1660. So he borrowed money from his friend, Admiral William Penn. King Charles never forgot his friend's loyalty.

King Charles did not repay his loan. However, he gave Penn's son, also named William Penn, land in North America in 1681. King Charles asked Penn to name the colony Pennsylvania, meaning "Penn's woods" to honor Penn's father.

Penn belonged to the Society of Friends. Members of the Society were jailed and even killed because of their beliefs. Penn decided that in his colony, all people could worship without fear. He called Pennsylvania a **Holy Experiment** to prove that people of different beliefs could live together.

In 1682 Penn wrote *The Frame of the Government of Pennsylvania*. This government plan included freedom of worship and the right to a trial by jury.

▼ **Many of the German settlers of Pennsylvania were hard-working and successful farmers.**

William Penn advertised his colony in England and other places in Europe. He told of religious freedom, cheap land, and fortunes to be had. Thousands of people from England and Wales moved there. The journey across the Atlantic Ocean was dangerous. However, in their new home, they earned more money. One colonist wrote that poor people "get three time the Wages for their Labor" than in England.

Many Germans came to Pennsylvania. In Germany, wars had destroyed the land. There was not enough food to eat. Some of the Germans who came here were Mennonites. They were a religious group who dressed very simply.

In the German language, the word *Deutsch* means "German." It sounds like the English word *Dutch*. So descendants of German settlers are called Pennsylvania Dutch to this day.

Pennsylvania attracted many Scots-Irish. They were people from Scotland who settled in Ireland in the early 1600s. They did not find freedom or prosperity in Ireland. In Pennsylvania, many Scots-Irish lived in the edges of colonial settlements.

Pennsylvania bordered New York colony. Part of the New York colony reached the Atlantic Ocean. William Penn wanted Pennsylvania to have a port on the ocean. He wanted the part of the New York colony called the Three Lower Counties.

Penn bought this land from the Duke of York, another friend of his father. The land is now the state of Delaware. The colonists of the Three Lower Counties were Dutch, Swedish, and Finnish. They wanted to make laws for themselves. In 1702 Penn let this area make its own laws. However, Pennsylvania's governor ruled Delaware until 1776.

Religion in the American Colonies

Religion played an important part in England's North American colonies.

▲ Colonists on their way to church

Many colonists in North America wanted to be free to practice their religion. They did not have this freedom back home. Other colonists made strict rules regarding religion.

The Puritans—Massachusetts

The Puritans wanted to separate from the Church of England. In England, they were persecuted, or punished for their beliefs. In North America, the Puritans set up the Massachusetts Bay Colony. They did not allow people with other beliefs to live there. They did not allow women to be equal to men.

At a Glance: Religion in Five American Colonies

Colony	Founded By	Religion	Allowed Other Religions?
Virginia	Virginia Company	Church of England	No
Massachusetts	Separatists	Purified Church of England	No
Rhode Island	Roger Williams	Any	Yes
Maryland	Calvert Family	Catholic; Church of England	Of all Christians
Pennsylvania	William Penn	Any	Yes

The Quakers—Pennsylvania

Quakers' beliefs differed from the Puritans'. Quakers did not have priests and ministers. They believed that governments should not tell people what religion to practice. These ideas got them in trouble with the Puritans in Massachusetts.

In Pennsylvania, a colony founded by Quaker William Penn, all religions that believed in God had respect for each other.

Catholic Church—Maryland

In Europe, Catholics and Protestants were enemies. The Calvert family, who founded Maryland, was Catholic. However, in 1649, Maryland extended freedom of religion to Protestants.

Church of England—Virginia

In Virginia, all colonists had to belong to the Church of England. Virginia colonists had to convert Native Americans to Christianity. The most famous convert was Pocahontas. *—Lisa Jo Rudy*

The Granger Collection

▲ A Quaker meeting in Philadelphia

Jews in Rhode Island

Puritan minister Roger Williams lived in the Massachusetts colony. In 1638, he was expelled after a disagreement with the colony's leaders. He founded Rhode Island, a colony open to all religions. In 1658, Jews arrived in Newport, Rhode Island, seeking freedom of religion. They built Touro Synagogue. It was the first lasting Jewish synagogue in America.

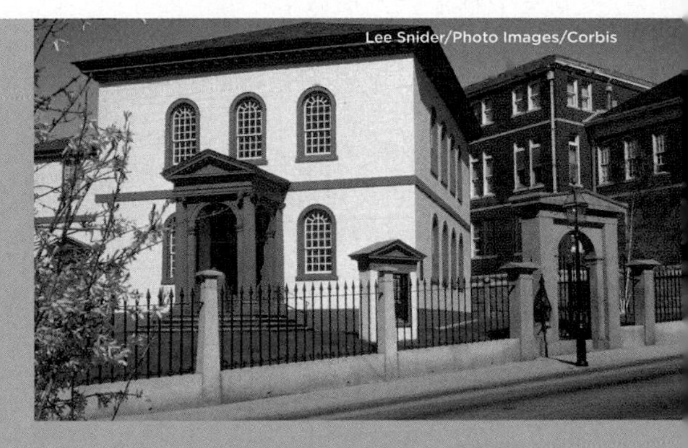

Lee Snider/Photo Images/Corbis

▲ Touro Synagogue today

Problem/Solution Writing Frame

Use the Writing Frame below to orally summarize "William Penn Founds a Colony."

In England, members of the Society of Friends were jailed and even killed for their beliefs. **To help solve this problem**, William

Penn ____

____

____

____.

Penn needed land in North America for his new colony. **To solve this problem**, Penn got land from ______________________.

The result was a colony where people of different beliefs ______________

____.

Use the frame to write the summary on another sheet of paper. Be sure to include the **bold** signal words. Keep this as a model of this Text Structure.

Critical Thinking

1. The colony called a Holy Experiment was named ______________.

   A. Delaware

   B. Pennsylvania

   C. New York

2. Find the meaning of *revolution* in "William Penn Founds a Colony."

3. Locate the paragraph in "Religion in the American Colonies" that tells who founded Maryland.

4. Review the chart on page 128. Discuss with a partner which colonies probably had the most people from different religions and why.

Charts may show different categories to help the reader organize information.

Digital Learning

For a list of links and activities that relate to this History/Social Science standard, visit the California Treasures Web site at www.macmillanmh.com to access the Content Readers resources. Have students view the Biography "Anne Hutchinson."

SELF-GOVERNMENT

Colonies needed laws. Each colony elected an **assembly**, or lawmaking body. Each colony's charter allowed the colony to have an assembly. Virginia formed the first assembly, called the House of Burgesses, in 1619.

The assemblies met to make and pass laws. This is called **legislation**. Even though the assemblies' laws helped the colonists govern themselves, a governor or leaders in London had to approve all laws.

The assemblies decided how to spend the colony's money. They determined how much to pay colonial officials.

In order to join the assembly, a colonist had to run for election—and win. At first, only white males who owned land were allowed to run for office and to vote.

Later a small number of men who did not own land could vote and be elected to assemblies. Women, indentured servants, enslaved Africans, and Native Americans were not allowed to vote or hold office.

Because members of assemblies were elected, they were popular with the colonists and represented their views. Colonial assemblies modeled themselves on the English lawmaking body, called Parliament. Colonists considered themselves to be free English citizens.

Colonists elected members of the assembly, but they did not elect their governors. The king or the colony's proprietor, or owner, usually chose the governors. Only Connecticut and Rhode Island elected their own governors.

The king and proprietors chose colonial governors carefully. They wanted governors who obeyed them. For this reason, most governors were unpopular with colonists.

The governor had the power to reject any law passed by a colonial assembly. When this happened, the assembly was allowed to ask the English government in London for help. The governor had to explain to the king or proprietor why he rejected the law.

An early colonial assembly meets. ▶

Some colonial governors had the power to stop assemblies from meeting. However, governors had to get along with their assemblies. After all, the governor needed assembly-controlled money to run the colony.

The assembly handled matters that concerned the entire colony. Other colonial officials helped govern towns and counties.

The colonies also had courts. Justices, or judges, supervised colonial courts. Local courts settled disputes and answered questions about the law.

Each county had a sheriff to enforce laws. A lawbreaker often had to spend time in the public **pillory**. A pillory is a wooden frame with holes for a person's neck and hands. The pillory was meant to embarrass people who were found guilty of minor offenses such as swearing. Whipping or even death were possible punishments for serious crimes such as robbery.

Colonial elections were much different from today's elections. Candidates spoke to colonists one at a time. Candidates were also expected to "treat," or buy food for voters. On Election Day, voters in some colonies had to sign their names on their ballots. This kept people from voting more than once, but it enabled others to see the names of the people they had voted for.

A slave pen like the one recreated at the museum

(t) Courtesy National Underground Railroad Freedom Center, (inset) Layne Kennedy/CORBIS

Honoring Freedom

This museum tells the story of a quest for freedom.

The National Underground Railroad Freedom Center honors the people who helped slaves find freedom. The museum is in Cincinnati, Ohio, across the Ohio River from Kentucky, a former slave state.

Slavery in the United States

Starting in the 1600s, millions of people were kidnapped from their homes in Africa. They were brought to North America as slaves. Slavery continued for more than 200 years, even after the colonies became the United States.

Enslaved people had no rights. Families were torn apart when slaves were sold. Slaves were often abused. They were not allowed to receive an education.

However, thousands of brave men and women risked their lives to help enslaved people find freedom. Because of their efforts, many slaves escaped or resisted their masters.

Courtesy National Underground Railroad Freedom Center

Bettmann/Corbis

A slave market

Cruel Reminder—The Slave Pen

At the museum, visitors can enter a slave pen that was once used to lock up dozens of people as they waited to be sold. Wooden structures like this were once found throughout the upper South.

Make a Difference

At the Freedom Center's Hall of Everyday Heroes, visitors learn about people who helped others find freedom. Naomi Nelson is the center's director of education. She hopes that the museum shows people that they can stand up and make a difference. *—Susan Moger*

Former Slaves Speak

In the 1930s, more than 2,300 people who had once been enslaved were interviewed as part of the Federal Writers' Project.

These selections are from their stories.

Marilda Pethy, no age given
"Why, I've seen people handcuffed together and driven . . . like cattle. . . . I had two brothers and two sisters sold, and we never did see them [again]. . . . "

Sarah Frances Shaw Graves, age 87
"I was born March 23, 1850, in Kentucky, somewhere near Louisville. I was brought to Missouri when I was six months old, along with my mama. . . . We left my papa in Kentucky. . . . My papa never knew where my mama went, and my mama never knew where papa went."

John W. Fields, age 89
"Plantation owners were very harsh if we were caught trying to learn or write."

Description Writing Frame

Use the Writing Frame below to orally summarize "Honoring Freedom."

Slavery in the United States has a sad and terrible history.

For example, enslaved people had no ______________________________.

Families were ____

____.

Also, slaves were not allowed to ______________________________

____.

Slaves were often abused. **For example**, many slave owners

in the upper South had slave pens. **They were used** to ______________

____.

To help enslaved people, thousands ______________________________

____.

Use the frame to write the summary on another sheet of paper. Be sure to include the **bold** signal words. Keep this as a model of this Text Structure.

Critical Thinking

1. A lawmaking body is called an ________________.

   A. legislation

   B. assembly

   C. colony

2. Point to the sentence in "Self-Government" that describes the first voters.

3. Reread the paragraph in "Self-Government" that explains lawbreakers' punishment in the colonies.

4. Orally create your own caption for the photo of the slave pen on page 134.

Captions give the reader additional information about the subject of the article.

Digital Learning

For a list of links and activities that relate to this History/Social Science standard, visit the California Treasures Web site at www.macmillanmh.com to access the Content Readers resources. Have students read "Enslaved Young People in the Colonies During the 1700s."

PROTESTING NEW TAXES

The British government had spent a lot of money protecting colonists during the French and Indian War. After the war ended in 1763, King George III and his advisors made a plan for the colonists to pay for some of the war costs. Parliament, the British legislature, introduced new taxes that the colonists had to pay.

In 1764 the British government passed the **Sugar Act**. It required colonists to pay a tax on all sugar products. People who did not pay the tax were arrested and fined.

In 1765 the British government passed the **Stamp Act** which affected all printed items. Every letter, newspaper, pamphlet, and legal document had to have an official stamp. Colonists paid for the stamps.

The colonists did not get to vote on these acts. They were against giving the money to Great Britain, rather than to the colonial government.

A few months later, the British government passed the **Quartering Act**. This act said that colonists had to let British soldiers stay in their homes if the colonists were asked to do so.

Colonial leaders and everyday citizens protested the acts. In October 1765, representatives from nine colonies met in New York City. Their meeting became known as the Stamp Act Congress.

The representatives pointed out that colonists were not allowed to vote for members of Parliament. According to the representatives, this is why Parliament did not have the right to tax the colonists.

The day after the Stamp Act went into effect, almost all colonists boycotted the stamps. To **boycott** means to refuse to do business with—or to buy or use goods from—a person, group, or country.

Men and women stopped buying tea and other British goods. The boycott hurt British merchants. In 1766, Parliament voted to **repeal**, or end, the Stamp Act.

In 1767 Parliament passed the **Townshend Acts**. These acts ordered taxes to be paid on goods made in Great Britain such as paper, glass, lead, and paint.

The colonists knew they had power when they worked together. They agreed to boycott the new taxed items. They also refused to do business with people who did not participate in the boycott.

The British government repealed the Townshend Acts, but it passed the Tea Act in March of 1773. **The Tea Act** put a tax on tea sold by colonial merchants. The act also removed the tax on tea sold by the British East India Company. As a result, British tea was less expensive than tea sold by colonial merchants.

The Boston Tea Party

In late November 1773, three British East India Company ships entered Boston Harbor. The ships carried tea. Colonists refused to let the ships' crews bring the tea to shore. The governor of Massachusetts, Thomas Hutchinson, ordered the ships to stay in the harbor until the tea was sold.

On the night of December 16, 1773, about 50 colonists boarded the ships. They called themselves Sons of Liberty. Some were disguised as Mohawk Indians. They opened the tea chests and emptied the tea into the harbor. This attack became known as the Boston Tea Party.

Parliament punished the colonists of Boston. Boston Harbor was closed until the colonists paid for the tea. Town meetings were not allowed. Colonists called Parliament's actions the Intolerable Acts. *Intolerable* means "unbearable." The Intolerable Acts brought the colonies together to fight against Great Britain.

Representatives of the colonies met in Philadelphia in September 1774 to discuss the problem. This meeting became known as the First Continental Congress.

The Congress sent King George III a **petition**, or written request signed by many people. In their petition, the Congress asked the king to repeal the Intolerable Acts.

The Congress also agreed to boycott trade with Great Britain again. Colonists feared a British attack. Each colony was asked to organize groups of **minutemen**. Minutemen were men who promised to assemble at a minute's notice to defend their towns.

People in the colonies communicated by writing letters. People shared their ideas and worries by writing. The colonists knew they had difficult choices to make.

How They Chose These Words for the Declaration of Independence

The writing of the Declaration of Independence was assigned to Thomas Jefferson, but he had some help.

In 1776 the Continental Congress prepared to vote on whether the colonies should break free of Great Britain to become independent. Before voting, Congress needed a written declaration to explain the decision.

Bettmann/Corbis

Congress chose a group of people to write the Declaration of Independence. Thomas Jefferson was the chairman of the committee. It became his job to write the first draft of the declaration. Why? Other members of the committee were busy with other work. Benjamin Franklin was sick in bed.

So Jefferson sat down to write the Declaration of Independence. He started with the words "When in the course of human events . . ."

His writing criticized the King of England. In those days, such writing meant you were declaring a revolution.

Bettmann/Corbis

▲ **Thomas Jefferson**

Jefferson took many ideas and words from other writers like Benjamin Franklin and the philosopher John Locke. He even copied parts of the Declaration of Rights from the Constitution of Virginia.

Once he finished his draft, Jefferson showed it to Franklin. Franklin made some changes. He rewrote "We hold these truths to be sacred and undeniable" as "We hold these truths to be self-evident." This is one of the Declaration's most famous sentences.

On July 2, 1776, the Continental Congress read Jefferson's Declaration. They made a great many changes, and Jefferson was quite upset. Finally, the document was complete.

The official signing of the Declaration of Independence took place on August 2. John Hancock, the president of the Congress, signed his name boldly. "There must be no pulling different ways," he declared. "We must all hang together." According to the early American historian Jared Sparks, Franklin replied, "Yes, we must, indeed, all hang together, or most assuredly we shall all hang separately." *—Lisa Jo Rudy*

▼ **The signed Declaration of Independence**

IN CONGRESS, JULY 4, 1776.

The unanimous Declaration of the thirteen united States of America.

NARA

Cause/Effect Writing Frame

Use the Writing Frame below to orally summarize "Protesting New Taxes."

There were several **causes** for the colonists' boycott of British goods.

After the French and Indian War, King George III and his advisors

wanted colonists in North America to ______________________.

To do this, the British government passed ______________________.

A few months later, the British passed the Quartering Act. This

caused people in the colonies to ______________________

______________________.

As a result of the colonists' actions, British merchants ______________________

______________________.

The passing of the Tea Act repealed ______________________

______________________.

As a result of the Boston Tea Party, Parliament passed ______________________

______________________.

For all of these reasons the colonists agreed to boycott.

Use the frame to write the summary on another sheet of paper. Be sure to include the **bold** signal words. Keep this as a model of this Text Structure.

Critical Thinking

1 The _______________ Acts taxed goods made in Great Britain.

A. Tea

B. Townshend

C. Quartering

2 Point to the sentence in "Protesting New Taxes" that provides a definition of the word *repeal*.

3 Locate the paragraph in "How They Chose These Words for the Declaration of Independence" that explains why Jefferson's words meant he was declaring a revolution.

4 Review the painting of the Boston Tea Party on page 139. Discuss with a partner how this picture and caption explain the text.

Illustrations and captions give visual examples that help explain what the text states.

Digital Learning

For a list of links and activities that relate to this History/Social Science standard, visit the California Treasures Web site at www.macmillanmh.com to access the Content Readers resources. Have students view "The Struggle for North America."

AMERICANS OF THE REVOLUTION

The war between Great Britain and its 13 colonies is called the **American Revolution**. Here are two Americans from that time who shaped the new nation.

Abigail Adams 1744–1818

Abigail Smith lived in a time when many girls did not go to school. Her father encouraged Abigail to read about any subject she liked. She read about many things.

In 1764 Smith married John Adams. In 1797 John Adams became the second President of the United States. Abigail Adams wrote her husband hundreds of letters while he was away from home. Her letters told about events. In her letters, she also gave him political advice.

Adams was against slavery. She also believed women should have the same rights as men. She wanted all girls to be able to go to school. She once wrote her husband, "Remember the ladies, and be more generous and favorable to them than your ancestors."

The Life of Abigail Adams

1740 | 1760 | 1780 | 1800 | 1820

- 1744 Born in Weymouth, Mass.
- 1764 Marries John Adams
- 1774 Manages family farm
- 1800 Moves to the White House
- 1818 Dies in Quincy, Mass.

The Life of George Washington

1730	1740	1750	1760	1770	1780	1790	1800

- 1732 Born in Virginia, February 22
- 1775 Becomes commander in chief of the Continental army
- 1789 Becomes the first President of the United States
- 1799 Dies on December 14

George Washington 1732–1799

"I cannot tell a lie!" young George Washington told his father. Then he confessed to cutting down his father's cherry tree.

This famous story about George Washington is not true! It seems someone made it up to show that honesty was always important to him. When he was about 12 years old, he copied 110 rules for "good behavior" in his notebook. He wrote, "Be Careful to keep your Promise."

Washington was a young man when the French and Indian War started. Governor Dinwiddie of Virginia put him in command of Virginia's troops. Washington was a brave leader and an honest, caring man.

In 1775 the Continental Congress elected Washington commander in chief of the Continental army. His soldiers trusted him even when he was discouraged. In 1789, six years after the American Revolution, Washington became the first President of the United States.

The (Federalist) Party's Over

The Federalist party ruled for a while—then it disappeared.

Bettmann/Corbis

▲ George Washington, a Federalist, is sworn in as President of the United States.

In the late 1700s Federalist Party leaders ruled the new United States of America. George Washington, Alexander Hamilton, and John Adams were all Federalists.

By 1800, though, most people thought Federalists cared only for themselves. So Republicans (not the same as today's Republicans) became powerful. Federalists were important only in New England.

Then a war started between Britain and France. United States leaders did not want to join the war. However, in 1812, Republican President James Madison declared war on Britain. He wanted the British navy to stop taking goods and sailors from American ships.

Federalists were against this war, the War of 1812. They did not think the new country was ready to fight it. They worried that Britain would stop doing business with the United States.

The War of 1812 brought both successes and defeats for the United States. American frigates beat British ships. The British took over Detroit and burned Washington. They prepared to attack New Orleans.

Bettmann/Corbis

Washington, D.C., was burned by the British in 1814. ▶

The United States was in real danger. Some Federalists wanted New England and New York to separate from the rest of the states. Other Federalists wanted to use federal tax dollars to pay for defending their states. They also wanted to pass a law that said citizens could not be forced to serve in the war.

These Federalists did not have time to present their ideas. The war had already come to an end.

Federalists gained a bad reputation because they did not support the war. Today, the Federalist Party doesn't exist.

The Granger Collection, NYC

▲ The Treaty of Ghent, signed in 1814, ended the war.

◀ American and British ships battled during the War of 1812.

Francis G. Mayer/Corbis

Sequence Writing Frame

Use the Writing Frame below to orally summarize "The (Federalist) Party's Over."

In the late 1700s, leaders from the Federalist Party ruled the new United States of America.

By 1800, most people thought the Federalists ____________________

____.

After that, the Republicans ____________________________.

Then a war began between ____________________________.

In 1812, President James Madison decided to ____________________

____.

During the war some Federalists wanted ____________________

____.

Federalists gained a bad reputation because they ____________________

____.

Today, the Federalist Party ____________________________.

Use the frame to write the summary on another sheet of paper. Be sure to include the **bold** signal words. Keep this as a model of this Text Structure.

Critical Thinking

1. George Washington, Alexander Hamilton, and John Adams were ________________.

   A. Federalists

   B. Republicans

   C. Democrats

2. Find the sentence in "Americans of the Revolution" that explains what Abigail Adams thought about slavery.

3. Find the paragraph in "The (Federalist) Party's Over" that describes some of the successes and defeats of the War of 1812.

4. Study the time line on page 145. Was George Washington a young man when he became President? Discuss with a partner.

Time lines present events in time-order.

Digital Learning

For a list of links and activities that relate to this History/Social Science standard, visit the California Treasures Web site at www.macmillanmh.com to access the Content Readers resources. Have students read the Biography "Abigail Adams."

THE WAR BEGINS

The war between Great Britain and its former colonies started in 1775. The fighting lasted eight long and deadly years.

Americans who supported the Revolution were called **Patriots**. During the war, Patriot men became soldiers. Most of them were young and did not have experience. Many African Americans became soldiers. They hoped that slavery would end if the United States won the war. Women also helped. Some went to the battlefields to work as cooks or nurses. Others tended farms or shops.

Great Britain was a very powerful enemy. Its army was strong. Patriots from different states had to find a way to work together.

Each colony was now an independent state. Each state needed a government. So each state held a formal meeting to write a constitution, or plan of government. The meeting was called a **convention**.

The new country also needed a national government for all the states. During the war, the Second Continental Congress took on this role. In 1777 the Continental Congress passed the Articles of Confederation, the first written plan for an American government.

The Articles of Confederation gave state governments more power than the national government. The Continental Congress could not vote for taxes. It also did not have the power to tell states to send soldiers or supplies for the war.

At the beginning of the war, the weak Continental Congress made it easier for the British to fight the Patriots. However, the Patriots fought to be free. Their desire for independence helped them win important battles.

On December 25, 1776, George Washington led 2,400 soldiers across the Delaware River. Washington's army reached Trenton, New Jersey, at dawn. They quickly attacked the enemy. Washington's army forced the Hessians, German soldiers who helped the British, to surrender. Then the Americans defeated the British at Princeton, New Jersey, on January 2, 1777.

The British found out they would not win the war easily. In 1777 they made a new plan. The British decided to capture the Hudson River Valley. This would make it difficult for New York and New Jersey Patriots to get supplies.

In late summer, British General John Burgoyne led his troops south from Canada toward New York. As they traveled, Burgoyne learned that Native American allies like the Iroquois and Mohawks no longer wanted to help the British. The Native Americans used to gather information about the American troops. When they stopped believing the British could help them keep their lands, the scouting stopped. As a result, Burgoyne did not know that American troops led by General Horatio Gates were preparing for battle.

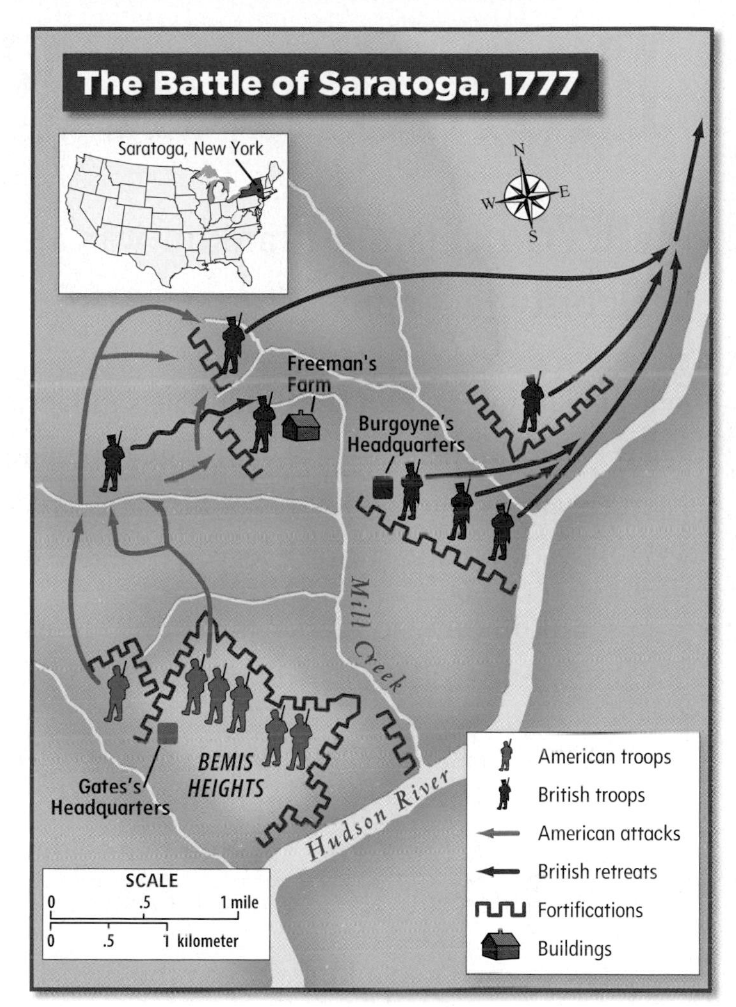

The American army waited near Saratoga, New York. They had nearly three times as many soldiers as the British. In addition, Gates had sent out groups of Virginia soldiers to make constant surprise attacks on the British. These attacks weakend the British as they approached Saratoga.

In September 1777, Burgoyne's troops began a two-month battle against American soldiers at Saratoga. By October the British were almost out of food. Burgoyne was losing men daily to riflemen hidden in the hillsides. His troops surrendered on October 17, 1777.

The American victory at Saratoga helped convince Europeans to help the United States. In February 1778, the French and American governments signed a **Treaty of Alliance**. This was a formal agreement to work together. French troops and supplies began to arrive in the United States.

Franklin in France

In 1776 Benjamin Franklin was an American celebrity in France.

Bettmann/Corbis

▲ **Benjamin Franklin**

Benjamin Franklin arrived in Paris in December 1776. People wanted to meet him. They applauded him in the streets and theaters. Pictures of him appeared on clocks, rings, and walking sticks. Everyone wanted his portrait.

Franklin came to France to ask the French for war supplies. Americans needed guns and gunpowder to fight the British.

In some ways, Franklin's job was easy. The French were not British allies. Also, the French thought they might make a fortune by trading with the Americans. On the other hand, Franklin represented people who had different views from the French.

The French had a king, just as the British did. The Americans believed kings were tyrants. French aristocrats believed they were born into families that had a right to be rich. Americans believed that all men were created equal.

The Granger Collection

Paris in the late 1760s

Franklin was 70 years old and not exactly handsome. The French thought he was wonderful all the same.

Many French people thought that Franklin was a general. However, he never fought in a war. They thought he was a farmer, though he'd always lived in cities. He wore a raccoon cap to make himself look like a pioneer, but he never traveled into the frontier. The French believed Franklin was a Quaker, though he was not.

After eight years in France, Franklin achieved his goals. He worked out American treaties with France. The Treaty of Paris, signed in 1783, was the key to making the United States an independent nation. *—Lisa Jo Rudy*

Northwind Picture Archives

▲ **Franklin was treated like a celebrity in Paris.**

Northwind Picture Archives

▲ **Franklin at the French royal court**

Description Writing Frame

Use the Writing Frame below to orally summarize "Franklin in France."

The French treated Benjamin Franklin like a celebrity.

When he arrived in Paris in December 1776, they ______________________

____.

Franklin came to France to ______________________________

____.

On the other hand, Franklin represented ______________________

____.

The French believed things about Franklin that were not true,

such as ____

____.

In France, Franklin achieved goals **such as** ______________________

____.

Use the frame to write the summary on another sheet of paper. Be sure to include the **bold** signal words. Keep this as a model of this Text Structure.

Critical Thinking

1 The Treaty of Alliance was signed by the ________________ and American governments.

A. British

B. Native American

C. French

2 Find the word in "The War Begins" that means "a formal meeting."

3 Point to the paragraph in "Franklin in France" that explains why Franklin came to France.

4 Review the map on page 151. Were the British and American fortifications far apart? Use the map scale. Discuss your findings with a partner.

The scale shows the relationship between distances on a map and real distances.

Digital Learning

For a list of links and activities that relate to this History/Social Science standard, visit the California Treasures Web site at www.macmillanmh.com to access the Content Readers resources. Have students read the Biography "George Washington."

LIFE DURING THE AMERICAN REVOLUTION

American women found many ways to fight the war. Martha Washington, wife of the commander in chief, often visited her husband and his men on the battlefield. She helped the sick and wounded. Martha Washington, Sarah Osborn, and other patriot women helped to keep farms working while their husbands and fathers were at war.

Some women fought in the Continental army. Deborah Sampson and Margaret Corbin dressed like men to join the army. Mary Ludwig Hays McCauley carried pitchers of water to thirsty soldiers during battle. That is why they called her Molly Pitcher. When her husband was wounded during the Battle of Monmouth, she took his place. Lydia Darragh and Martha Bell were patriot spies.

Other women wrote books, pamphlets, poems, and letters. Their writing inspired Americans to continue to fight. Poet Phillis Wheatley wrote poems about freedom. Mercy Otis Warren wrote a book about the American Revolution. Abigail Adams was married to political leader John Adams. In her letters, she gave him advice. She formed a group that got people to give money for soldiers in the Continental army.

Molly Pitcher loaded the cannon during the Battle of Monmouth, New Jersey.

During the war, many American people did not have enough food, clothing, and other goods. Items such as cloth, kettles, and tools used to come from Great Britain.

Hoarding caused other shortages. Hoarding is hiding away important goods. Such goods included flour, molasses, cotton cloth, clothing, and certain household tools. Some businesses and farmers began **profiteering**, or raising prices, of goods. New laws tried to stop profiteering. However, the laws were difficult to enforce. As a result, the price of many products rose sharply.

The cost of war supplies also increased. To pay for them, Congress printed more and more paper money. These paper bills were called Continentals. So many Continentals were printed that they began to lose value.

The drop in the value of Continentals caused **inflation**. Inflation is a large and rapid increase in prices. For example, a musket that had cost five Continentals soon cost 12 Continentals. By the end of the war, a pair of shoes cost 5,000 Continentals.

▲ It took more Continental dollars to buy the same goods as the war continued.

Cause/Effect Writing Frame

Use the Writing Frame below to orally summarize "Life During the American Revolution."

The Revolution changed the daily life of the American people.

One effect of the American Revolution was that many people

did not have enough ______________________________.

Manufactured goods were hard to find **because** ______________________

____.

People who had important goods caused shortages by ________________

____.

In order to make more money, some businesses started ______________

____.

To pay for more expensive supplies, Congress ______________________

____.

So many Continentals were printed that it **caused** ____________________

______________________________. **The result was** inflation.

Use the frame to write the summary on another sheet of paper. Be sure to include the **bold** signal words. Keep this as a model of this Text Structure.

Critical Thinking

1. ________________ is a large and rapid increase in prices.

   A. Profiteering

   B. Hoarding

   C. Inflation

2. Point to the sentence in "Life During the American Revolution" that explains how Molly Pitcher received her name.

3. Did Martha Washington want her husband to be President? Locate the paragraph in "Martha Washington, America's *First* First Lady" that answers the question.

4. Review the illustrations and captions of Martha Washington on page 159. Discuss with a partner how her life changed after George became President.

Illustrations and captions give visual examples that help explain what the text states.

Digital Learning

For a list of links and activities that relate to this History/Social Science standard, visit the California Treasures Web site at www.macmillanmh.com to access the Content Readers resources. Have students view the video "The Struggle for North America."

PLANNING A NEW GOVERNMENT

In 1777 the Articles of Confederation set up the first government of the United States. The Articles of Confederation allowed each state to make its own laws, collect its own taxes, and print its own money. The national government was weak. This caused many problems. In 1786, Daniel Shays, a farmer in Massachusetts, got thousands of farmers to protest taxes. Many of the farmers were veterans of the American Revolution. They could not pay their taxes because Congress owed them money. A bloody battle, known as **Shays's Rebellion**, followed. Troops were called in.

On May 25, 1787, **delegates** from 12 states met at a convention in Philadelphia. A delegate represents other people by speaking for them and working to help them get what they want. Rhode Island was the only state that did not send any delegates. Its residents did not want the convention to take power from them.

James Madison arrived in Philadelphia with a new plan for a strong national government, called the **Virginia Plan**. Madison convinced most of the delegates that the Articles of Confederation were not enough. The meeting in Philadelphia was called the Constitutional Convention because it worked on a constitution for a new national government.

Delegates disagreed about the number of representatives each state would have. Roger Sherman, from Connecticut, suggested that the legislature have two parts.

In the **House of Representatives**, the number of representatives depended on the number of people who lived in a state. States with high populations had more representatives. These representatives would serve two years and be chosen directly by the people. States with fewer people had fewer representatives.

In the **Senate**, each state would have two members. They would serve six-year terms and be chosen by state legislatures. According to Sherman's plan, laws had to be approved by both the Senate and the House of Representatives.

▼ **John Hancock was the governor of Massachusetts during Shays's Rebellion.**

Sherman's plan was adopted on July 16, 1787. It became known as the **Great Compromise**. Delegates also had to decide how to choose the President of the United States. Some delegates did not trust the people to choose a good candidate. James Madison suggested that Congress pick the President.

The delegates compromised by creating the **Electoral College**. In the Electoral College, each state has a certain number of electoral votes. The vote is based on the number of representatives it has in Congress. A candidate must win a majority of the electoral votes to become President.

More than one third of the delegates at the Constitutional Convention owned plantations that used enslaved workers. Should the workers be counted as part of the population to determine how many representatives a state has? Some delegates said "no." Some delegates wanted an end to the slave trade. However, John Rutledge of South Carolina wanted to be sure that the slave trade be continued.

In the end, the delegates reached a compromise. Every five enslaved people in a state would be counted as three free people for state representation in Congress. The delegates also agreed to end slave trading with other countries in 1808.

On September 17, 1787, 39 delegates signed the Constitution. It had been a difficult struggle to reach an agreement.

When the Convention finished its work, Benjamin Franklin described the kind of government the delegates had prepared. Franklin said, "A republic, if you can keep it." The hard job of keeping the republic alive still lay ahead, and it continues to this day.

▼ **This painting of the signing of the Constitution is in the Capitol Building in Washington, D.C.**

How Free Are We to Speak Freely?

The First Amendment protects the right to free speech, but what free speech means is still being debated.

Alex Wong/Getty Images

Karen Bleier/AFP/Getty Images

▲ **Americans have the right to say what they think about government policies.**

Americans have the right to share our ideas, thanks to the First Amendment. The amendment is one of ten in the Bill of Rights, added to the Constitution in 1791.

The First Amendment is often amended. Court decisions have made changes to protect national security or the privacy of individuals, among other goals. However, freedom of speech is a fundamental right—and responsibility—of every American. This includes expressing your opinion about the government's policies.

The First Amendment

"Congress shall make no law respecting an establishment of religion, or prohibiting the free exercise thereof; or abridging the freedom of speech; or the right of the people peaceably to assemble, and to petition the government for a redress of grievances . . ."

Our right to free speech is protected in the Bill of Rights. ▶

NARA

Free Speech or Illegal Speech?

The First Amendment also protects written words. A very important part of that protection is freedom of the press. The "press" includes American journalists, whether writing for a newspaper, a magazine, or a Web site.

Still, there are certain types of speech that are never allowed. Some of these include

- **Treason.** Telling the enemy U.S. secrets is a crime that can be punished very severely.
- **Slander.** Saying untrue, negative things about another person in public is against the law.
- **Obscenity.** Obscene, or indecent, words and pictures are illegal.

Tricky Questions About Freedom of Speech

Are students on the property of public schools guaranteed the right of free speech?

In 2007 the Supreme Court decided a case about a student who had been suspended for holding up a sign outside a school. The sign said nothing illegal, but school officials said that its content was unacceptable. The court agreed with the school, but also added "while the court has limited student free speech rights in the past, young people do not give up all their First Amendment rights when they enter a school." Each case has to be decided one at a time. That is the job of the Supreme Court. *—Martha Pickerill and Susan Moger*

▲ **How free are students to speak freely?**

MOVING WEST

The American Revolution brought independence from Great Britain. Life was not easy for many people in the new nation. About one in five Americans lived in **poverty**. This means they did not have enough money for proper food or supplies. Many people made a living by farming the land they owned. However, not everyone had land. For many, life remained difficult.

Many farmers had large families. The children helped with the chores. When a farmer died, each of his children got some land. Often the land was not enough for the children to earn a living.

After the American Revolution, more babies were born. Many new people also came to the new nation. In 1790 the United States population was about 4 million. In 1820 it was 10 million. In the middle 1800s, the population grew even more as new people arrived. They included free blacks and enslaved African Americans.

Between 1845 and 1860, more immigrants came to the United States than ever before. Many Europeans came to find work. A million Irish people came to the United States to escape starvation. In the 1840s some people from China arrived. Later they worked on the railroads.

Some people settled in cities. Others moved to the open lands in the West. Poor people used these lands to improve their lives.

People found new routes to the West. This made it easier for people to travel. In 1769 a trader named John Findley wanted to find an inland trail from North Carolina to Kentucky. He chose experienced explorer Daniel Boone to help him. They found the Cumberland Gap, a natural passage through the Appalachian Mountains. The Wilderness Road was built through the gap. It became the main route for Americans heading west.

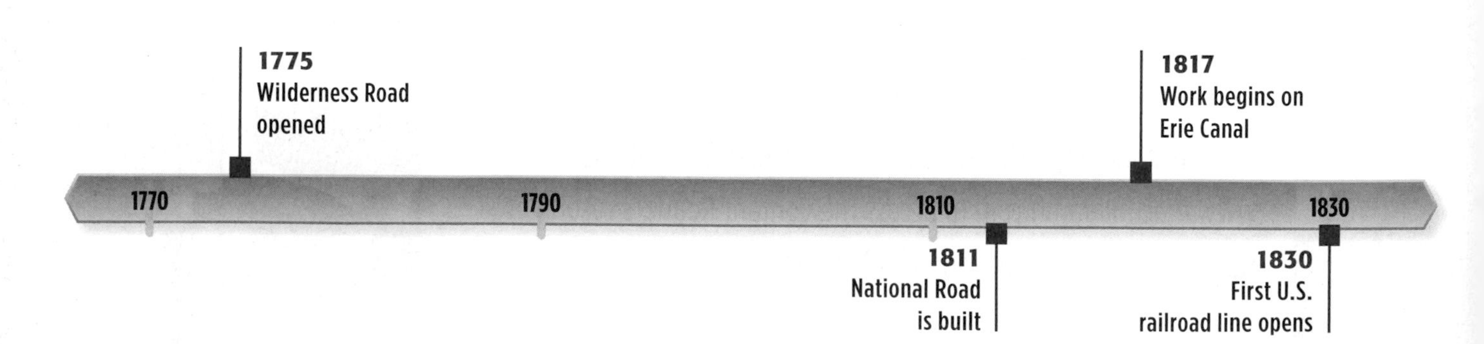

In the early 1800s, people traveled by **stagecoaches**—large, horse-drawn carriages. Travel was slow. Roads were dirt trails. They became muddy in the rain. They had potholes and tree stumps.

In 1811 America's first interstate highway, the National Road, opened. This stone road started in Cumberland, Maryland, and ended in Vandalia, Illinois—the western frontier.

People also traveled by boat. In August 1807, American inventor Robert Fulton revealed his *Clermont*, the first steamboat. It had a **steam engine**. Steam engines use stored up steam to produce motion.

The *Clermont* made the 150-mile trip up the Hudson River from New York City to Albany. It took 32 hours. Other boats needed 8 to 11 days to make the same trip.

By 1855 more than 700 steamboats traveled on rivers around the United States. Steamboats moved people and goods from place to place. People headed West and were able to bring or buy goods they needed.

People had traveled by railroad for years. At first, horses pulled the coaches over iron rails. In 1814 British inventor George Stephenson built the first train with a steam engine inside. People called these new trains "the iron horses."

In 1830 American merchant Peter Cooper built a small locomotive named *Tom Thumb*. Cooper raced his locomotive against a horse-drawn carriage. The little train lost the race. However, railroads became the main means of transportation in the nation.

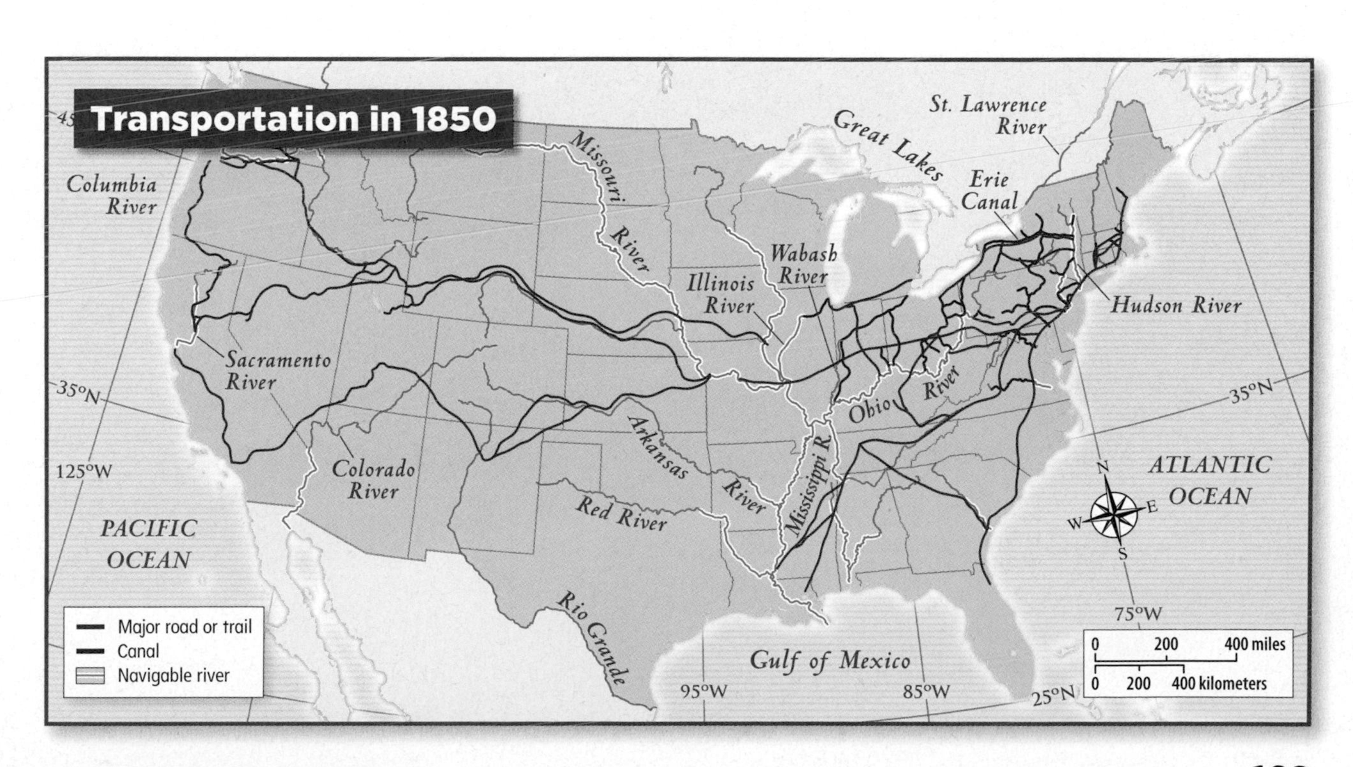

America in 1850

1850 was a challenging time for the United States.

Pioneers headed west during the 1850s. ▶

▲States and territories, 1850

In 1850 the United States was made of states and territories—areas that were not yet states. Most land west of Iowa and Wisconsin was a territory.

In some territories, pioneers and Native Americans clashed over land. New treaties spelled out who owned which land.

Brigham Young founded the Church of the Latter Day Saints (Mormons). He led his followers to Salt Lake City in the Utah territory to build their home.

In the West, thousands of people moved to California hoping to find gold. This period was called the Gold Rush. Thousands of people also moved to the Pacific Northwest. They traveled from Missouri along the Oregon Trail.

What About Slavery?

People did not agree about slavery in the United States in 1850. In the South, many believed that slaves were important to the growth of the nation. In the North, there were abolitionists, people who opposed slavery. Abolitionists wanted the United States to end slavery in all places. In 1850 some states, called slave states, allowed slavery. In the other states, called free states, slavery was illegal.

There was an equal number of slave and free states until California was ready to become a state. The balance between free and slave states was about to end. Senator Henry Clay of Kentucky offered a compromise. He suggested that California be named a free state. Meanwhile, new territories called New Mexico, Nevada, Arizona, and Utah would be neither free nor slave territories.

To get support from slave states, Clay proposed the Fugitive Slave Act. The law said that people had to help capture slaves who had run away. The law also said that caught slaves had no right to a jury trial. Congress accepted Clay's proposal, called the Compromise of 1850. California entered the Union as a free state. The harsh Fugitive Slave Act inspired abolitionists to fight harder to outlaw slavery—which happened in 1865.

▲Henry Clay argues for the California Compromise

People of the United States—1850 and Today

There are 11 times more people in the United States today than there were in 1850. However, about the same percentage of people are immigrants.

In 1850, more than 90 percent of immigrants came from Europe. Today only 23 percent of immigrants come from Europe. Instead, most immigrants come from Latin America and Asia. *—Lisa Jo Rudy*

In the News in 1850

- Women started campaigning for the right to vote.
- I. M. Singer and Company patented the first sewing machine.
- Joel Houghton invented the first automatic dishwasher.
- Levi Strauss began making blue jeans.

The Granger Collection

Sequence Writing Frame

Use the Writing Frame below to orally summarize "Moving West."

By 1820, the population of the United States grew ______________________

____.

Most farmers had large ______________________________.

Their children helped ______________________________.

In the middle 1800s, people from other countries ______________________

____.

Some of them settled in cities. Others ______________________.

People needed routes to reach the West. John Findley and

Daniel Boone ______________________________.

In the early 1800s, most people traveled by ______________________.

Travel by boat improved **when** Robert Fulton ______________________.

Railroad travel changed **after** George Stephenson ______________________

____.

Use the frame to write the summary on another sheet of paper. Be sure to include the **bold** signal words. Keep this as a model of this Text Structure.

Critical Thinking

1 In the early 1800's, most people traveled by ________________.

A. stagecoach

B. steamboat

C. railroad

2 Find the sentence in "Moving West" that explains how steam engines produce motion.

3 Find the paragraph in "America in 1850" that describes the reason for the Fugitive Slave Act.

4 Does the time line on page 168 provide any information that is not in the text? Discuss it with a partner.

A time line is a quick way to present a lot of information.

Digital Learning

For a list of links and activities that relate to this History/Social Science standard, visit the California Treasures Web site at www.macmillanmh.com to access the Content Readers resources. Have students view the video "A Nation Expands."

THE LOUISIANA PURCHASE

In 1803 the western border of the United States was the Mississippi River. President Thomas Jefferson wanted the United States to have more land. However, at the time, the French owned land west of the Mississippi. Their colony was called Louisiana. It stretched all the way to the Rocky Mountains, up to Canada, and down to the Gulf of Mexico.

Louisiana included New Orleans. Jefferson was worried that the French would stop the United States from trading there or from using the Mississippi River. His solution was to purchase Louisiana from the French.

France agreed to sell Louisiana. The United States bought the nearly 530 million acres for $15 million, or about $200 million in current dollars. Each acre cost about 3.5 cents. **The Louisiana Purchase** doubled the size of the United States.

Jefferson organized expeditions to explore the area. Jefferson selected Meriwether Lewis, his personal secretary, to lead the expedition. In June 1803, Lewis offered William Clark the chance to also be a leader of the famous expedition.

Meriwether Lewis (left) and William Clark (right) kept journals of plants and animals they studied.

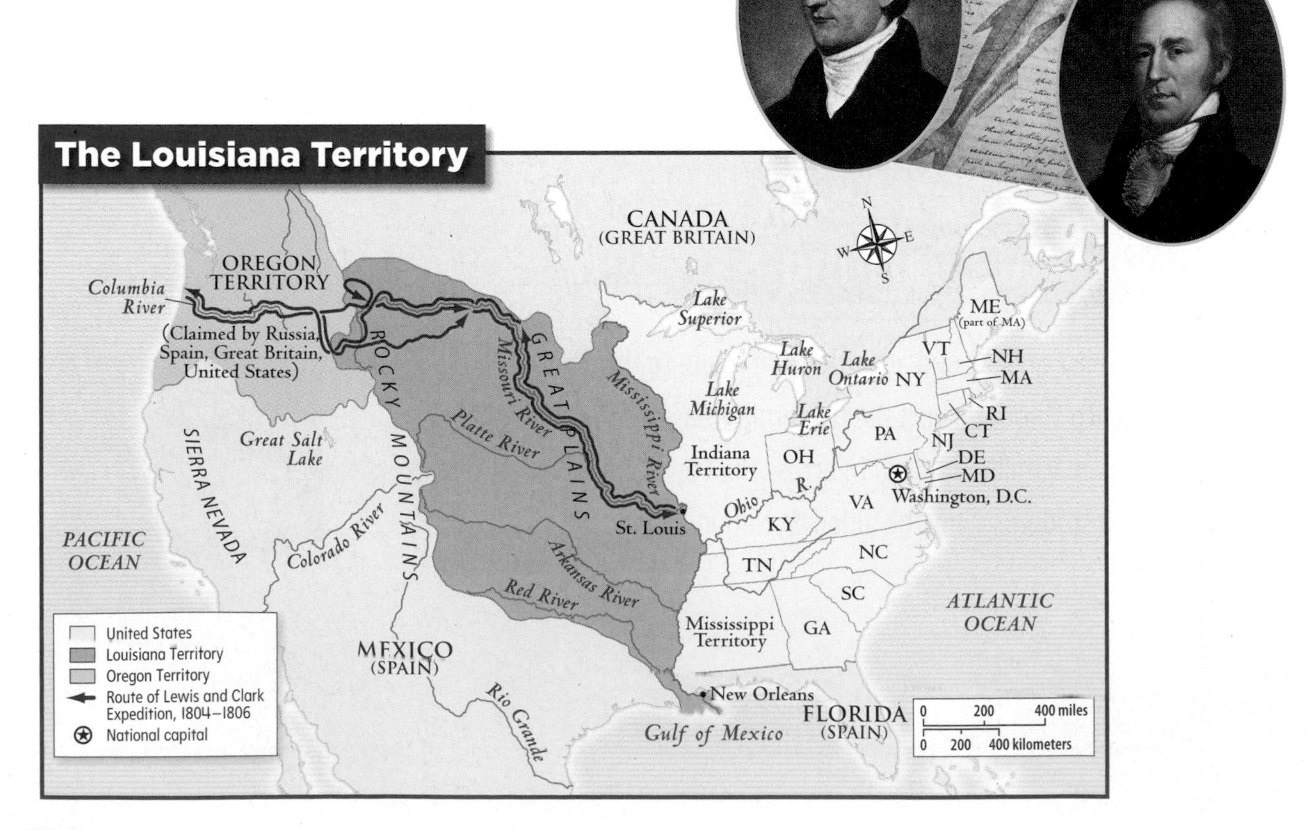

In May 1804, the Lewis and Clark Expedition started in St. Louis. They traveled west on the Missouri River. In 1805 a Shoshone woman, Sacagawea, became their main guide and interpreter. Led by Sacagawea and other Native American guides, the expedition traveled 8,000 miles. They crossed the Rocky Mountains and followed the Columbia River to the Pacific Ocean. They returned to St. Louis in 1806.

Jefferson sent other expeditions to the new territories. In 1805 Zebulon Pike searched for the source, or beginning, of the Mississippi River. He did not find it, but he did establish an American presence in the Louisiana Territory.

In another expedition, Pike reached the Rocky Mountains in the Oregon Territory. This territory included what are now Washington, Oregon, northern Idaho, part of Montana, and the Canadian province of British Columbia. He tried unsuccessfully to climb the mountain that is now called Pike's Peak.

The first settlers arrived in the Oregon Territory in the late 1830s. They were missionaries who tried to convert Native Americans to Christianity.

Letters from these missionaries told about the rich farmland of the Willamette Valley in Oregon. Midwestern farm families started moving to the West. Between 1841 and 1845, the American population of Oregon increased from 400 to 6,000.

Starting in 1841, people moving to Oregon traveled on the Oregon Trail. This wagon route connected Missouri to western Oregon. By 1860 more than 300,000 people had traveled on the Oregon Trail.

The settlers used covered wagons called Prairie Schooners. Smaller and lighter than other wagons, the Prairie Schooner still fit everything settlers needed.

It took about six months to travel the 2,000-mile route west. Most settlers joined a wagon train. When hundreds of wagons traveled together, the people were able to protect and help each other.

Everyone had a job to do. Men drove the wagons and repaired the equipment. Women cooked, set up tents, and washed clothes. Children hunted for buffalo chips, which were used as fuel for fires.

Problem/Solution Writing Frame

Use the Writing Frame below to orally summarize "A Historic Journey."

President Thomas Jefferson **wanted to** send ______________________________

____.

Jefferson **also wanted** the explorers to ______________________________

____.

An important member of the crew was a woman named ________________

____.

Lewis and Clark wrote in journals on the trip. While scouting,

Lewis **realized** ____

____.

To reach the coast, the explorers had to ___________________________

and ____.

Generations of Americans have declared the mission a success.

Use the frame to write the summary on another sheet of paper. Be sure to include the **bold** signal words. Keep this as a model of this Text Structure.

Critical Thinking

1 The Louisiana Purchase ______________ the size of the United States.

A. quadrupled

B. doubled

C. tripled

2 Find the sentence in "The Louisiana Purchase" that names the present-day areas that were part of the Oregon Territory.

3 Locate the sentence in "A Historic Journey" that explains what Lewis realized about the Northwest Passage.

4 Look at the map on page 174. With a partner, discuss Lewis and Clark's route.

The legend or key helps you understand the symbols on a map.

Digital Learning

For a list of links and activities that relate to this History/Social Science standard, visit the California Treasures Web site at www.macmillanmh.com to access the Content Readers resources. Have students view the Biography "Sacagawea."

THE UNITED STATES EXPANDS

After the Civil War, the United States gained the territories of **Alaska** and **Hawaii**. Other territories followed.

In the 1700s, Russia had a big colony in Alaska. It covered 500,000 square miles. Its people, especially the Inuit, had lived there for thousands of years. In 1867 Russia offered to sell Alaska to the United States. Secretary of State William Seward wanted the United States to pay $7.2 million for Alaska, or about 2 cents an acre. Some Americans thought the idea was a big mistake. They called Alaska "Seward's ice box" or "Seward's folly."

How wrong they were! In the 1880s, people found gold in the area that is now Juneau, Alaska's state capital. Alaska's plentiful resources also include fish, lumber, and oil.

The United States gained Hawaii in the 1890s. People had been living on these Pacific islands since between A.D. 600 and A.D. 1000. In 1778 an English sea captain, James Cook, went there. Christian missionaries arrived in the late 1820s.

By the 1890s, Americans had moved to Hawaii. Some built pineapple and sugarcane plantations. They became wealthy. **Queen Liliuokalani**, Hawaii's ruler, wanted to return power to native-born Hawaiians. In 1893 the American planters revolted. They took power from the queen. Then they asked the United States to let Hawaii become a state. At first, President Grover Cleveland refused. However, in 1898, Hawaii became a U.S. possession.

In 1959 Alaska became the forty-ninth state, and Hawaii became the fiftieth.

As a result of the **Spanish-American War** of 1898, the United States gained the islands of Puerto Rico, Guam, and the Philippines. Philippine rebels had been battling the Spanish when the United States took control of the Philippines.

Leader Emilio Aguinaldo and other Filipinos fought for independence until 1901. In 1946 the Philippines gained independence. However, both Guam and Puerto Rico have chosen to remain part of the United States. Their people are U.S. citizens.

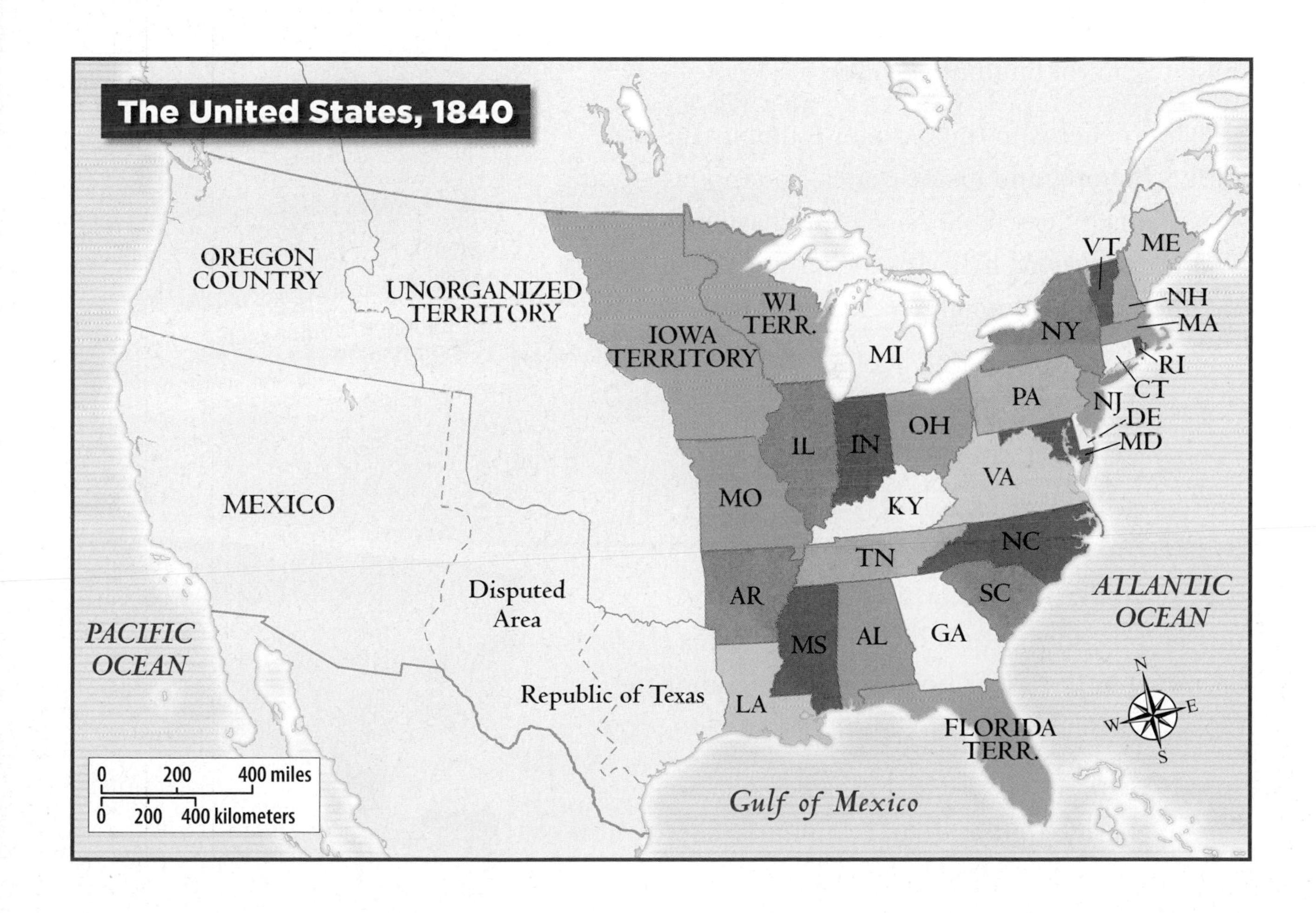

Some State Capital Snapshots

The cities that serve as state capitals are as different as the states they represent.

Montpelier, Vermont

Tiny Montpelier, Vermont, is the smallest state capital in the United States. Only about 8,000 residents live there. Its state capitol building, though, is famous.

Montpelier is in the Green Mountains. It has markets, shops, and historic sites—but no fast-food restaurants! Three U.S. Navy ships have been named *USS Montpelier*. Why? Montpelier was the birthplace of famous navy commander Admiral George Dewey.

Joseph Sohm/Visions of America/Corbis

▲ Vermont's impressive capitol building.

Sacramento, California

In 1849, the Gold Rush began in California. Sacramento became a boomtown. Even after the Gold Rush ended, Sacramento continued to grow.

Today there are about 450,000 people living in Sacramento, and more than 2 million in the metropolitan area. One landmark is the Tower Bridge between Sacramento and West Sacramento.

Gerald French/Corbis

▲ Sacramento's Tower Bridge

Denver, Colorado

Denver is called the Mile-High City because it is exactly one mile above sea level! It's the biggest town in Colorado. Over half a million people live there.

Denver has an average of 300 sunny days a year. Another cool Denver fact is that the roof of the Denver airport looks like the Rocky Mountains.

Bill Ross/Corbis

▲ Denver's skyline against the Rocky Mountains

Springfield, Illinois

Springfield is the birthplace of Abraham Lincoln. A new museum in Springfield tells his life story.

Springfield is the third city to be the capital of Illinois. The first capital was Kaskaskia. Then Vandalia became the capital. Finally, a group of legislators called the Long Nine got the capital moved to Springfield in 1839. The Long Nine got their name because all nine of them, including Lincoln, were over six feet tall!

Jason Reed/Corbis

▲ Springfield's Abraham Lincoln Presidential Library and Museum

Columbia, South Carolina

Columbia was founded in 1806, named for Christopher Columbus. In those days, landowners had to build a house at least 30 feet long and 18 feet wide within three years or pay a fine.

The city's planners made sure all streets were at least 100 feet wide. They believed mosquitoes couldn't fly 60 feet without starving to death!

Mary Ann Chastain/Ap Photo

▲ Columbia's African American History Monument

Compare/Contrast Writing Frame

Use the Writing Frame below to orally summarize "The United States Expands."

Alaska and Hawaii are **similar** in some ways. After the Civil War,

they **both** became ______________________________ of the United States.

They are **also alike because** in 1959 they both became ________________

____.

In some ways, however, Alaska and Hawaii **are different**.

In 1867, William Seward wanted the United States to ________________.

In comparison, in Hawaii in 1893 ____________________________________

____.

In 1898 ____.

So Alaska and Hawaii **are alike** in some ways and **different** in others.

Use the frame to write the summary on another sheet of paper. Be sure to include the **bold** signal words. Keep this as a model of this Text Structure.

Critical Thinking

1. Puerto Rico and ________________ have chosen to remain territories of the United States.

   A. Guam

   B. the Philippines

   C. Hawaii

2. Find the sentence in "The United States Expands" that names the last Queen of Hawaii.

3. Find the box of text in "Some State Capital Snapshots" that describes the Mile-High City. Discuss the text with a partner.

4. Study the map on page 181 with a partner. Name the states that were along the United States' border with the Republic of Texas and unorganized territory in 1840.

On maps, borders between states usually are drawn differently from the border between nations.

Digital Learning

For a list of links and activities that relate to this History/Social Science standard, visit the California Treasures Web site at www.macmillanmh.com to access the Content Readers resources. Have students view the video "The Nation Expands."

Illustration Acknowledgements

12, 24: Jeff Grunewald. 37: Linda Nye. 42: Bart Vallecoccia. 43: Laurie O' Keefe. 54: (bl) John Edwards. 55, 60, 72, 79, John Kauffman. 91: Jeff Grunewald

Photography Acknowledgements

All photos for Macmillan/McGraw-Hill except as noted below:

Cover: Alamy. 19: Oak Ridge National Laboratory. 25: Steve Raymer/National Geographic Image Collection/Getty Images. 30: Jim Zuckerman/CORBIS. 31: (tcl) Clouds Hill Imaging Ltd./CORBIS; (bcr) Michael Gabridge/Visuals Unlimited. 61: (tc) Lawrence Migdale/Photo Researchers. 85: NASA. 90: NASA/CORBIS. 102: Nationalmuseet Copenhagen Denmark/Dagli Orti (A)/The Art Archive. 114: North Wind Picture Archives. 118: North Wind Picture Archives. 121: The Granger Collection, New York. 126: Grant Heilman/Grant Heilman Photography. 133: North Wind Picture Archives. 139: The Granger Collection, New York. 144: The Granger Collection, New York. 145: Réunion des Musées Nationaux/Art Resource, NY. 156: The Granger Collection, New York. 157: (tr) The Granger Collection, New York; (t) The Granger Collection, New York. 162: (br) Bettmann/CORBIS; (b) The Granger Collection, New York. 174: (l to r) The Granger Collection, New York; National Historical Park, Independence, Missouri, MO, USA/ Bridgeman Art Library; The Granger Collection, New York